CONTEMPORARY GERMAN POETRY

An Anthology

Translated & Edited by

GERTRUDE CLORIUS SCHWEBELL

With an Introduction by Victor Lange

A NEW DIRECTIONS BOOK

New Directions Books are published for James Laughlin
by New Directions Publishing Corporation,
333 Sixth Avenue, New York 10014.

SECOND PRINTING

CONTENTS

v

ACKNOWLEDGMENTS

For permission to reprint copyright material, grateful acknowledgments are made: to Arche Verlag, Zurich, for the poems by Benn from *Statische Gedichte*, 1948; to Bechtle Verlag, Esslingen, for the poems by Piontek from *Die Rauchfahne*, 1953; by Heissenbüttel from *Kombinationen*, 1954; by Behnssen from *Lyrik aus dieser Zeit*, 1961; to Bergland Verlag, Vienna, for the poem by Lavant from *Tür an Tür*, 1955; to Claassen Verlag, Hamburg, for the poems by Kaschnitz from *Gedichte*, 1947, *Neue Gedichte*, 1957, *Dein Schweigen meine Stimme*, 1962; to Deutsche Verlags Anstalt, Stuttgart, for the poems by Celan from *Mohn und Gedächtnis*, 1952; by Krolow from *Die Zeichen der Welt*, 1952, *Wind und Zeit*, 1954; by Piontek from *Mit einer Kranichfeder*, 1962; by Meckel from *Nebelhörner*, 1959, *Wildnisse*, 1962; by Sachs from *Flucht und Verwandlung*, 1959; by Bobrowski from *Sarmatische Zeit*, 1961; to Eugen Diederichs Verlag, Düsseldorf-Cologne, for the poem by Miegel from *Gesammelte Gedichte*, 1952; to S. Fischer Verlag, Frankfurt am Main, for the poems by Domin from *Nur eine Rose als Stütze*, 1959, *Rückkehr der Schiffe*, 1961; by Huchel from *Gedichte*, 1948, *Chausseen Chausseen*, 1963; to Hanser Verlag, Munich, for the poem by Höllerer from *Der andere Gast*, 1952; by Bienek from *Traumbuch eines Gefangenen*, 1957; for the poems by Hädecke from *Leuchtspur im Schnee*, 1963; to Insel Verlag, Wiesbaden, for the poems by Hagelstange from *Zwischen Stern und Staub*, 1953; by Neumann from *Wind auf der Haut*, 1956; to Vittorio Klostermann, Frankfurt am Main, for the poems by Jünger from *Perlenschnur*, 1947, *Ring der Jahre*, 1954; to Kiepenheuer & Witsch, Cologne, for the poems by Bernhard from *Unter dem Eisen des Mondes*, 1958; to Limes Verlag, Wiesbaden, for the poems by Benn from *Gesammelte Gedichte*, 1956; by Arp from *Wortträume und schwarze Sterne*, 1953; to Hermann Luchterhand Verlag, Neuwied, for the poems by Grass from *Die Vorzüge der Windhühner*, 1956, *Gleisdreieck*, 1960; by Raeber from *Verwandelte Schiffe*, 1957; by Jokostra from *Magische Strasse*, 1960, *Hinab zu den Sternen*, 1961; to Sigbert Mohn Verlag, Gütersloh, for the poems by Lehmann from *Sämtliche Werke*, 1962; to Otto Müller Verlag, Salzburg, for the poems by Busta from *Die Scheune der Vögel*, 1958; by Lavant from *Die Bettlerschale*, 1956, *Spindel im Mond*, 1959; by Bernhard from *Auf der Erde und in der Hölle*, 1957; to R. Piper Verlag, Munich, for the poems by Holthusen from *Labyrinthische Jahre*, 1952; by Bachmann from *Anrufung des großen Bären*, 1956, *Die gestundete Zeit*, 1957; by Scharpenberg from *Gefährliche Übung*, 1957; to Lambert Schneider Verlag, Heidelberg, for the poems by Gong from *Gras und Omega*, 1960; to Suhrkamp Verlag, Frankfurt am Main, for the poems by Eich from *Botschaften des Regens*, 1955, *Ausgewählte Gedichte*, 1960; by Brecht from *Gedichte*, 1960-'61; by Krolow from *Fremde Körper*, 1959; for the poems by enzensberger from *verteidigung der wölfe*, 1957, *landessprache*, 1960, *Gedichte*, 1962; by Schröder from *Gesammelte Werke*, 1952-'63; to Stahlberg Verlag, Karlsruhe, for the poems by Huchel from *Gedichte*, 1948; to Tschudy & Co. Verlag, St. Gallen, Switzerland, for the poems by Hilty from *Eingebrannt in den Schnee*, 1957.

Acknowledgments are also made to the authors who hold their own copyrights: Bender for *Oktoberende, Gemeinsam, Der junge Soldat*; Brambach for *Hundstage, Paul*; Busta for *Jahreszeiten*; Gong for *Mars, Die fliegende Arche, Die Grenze, Erkenntnis*; Lavant for *Im hohlen Kern des Wirbelsturms*; Leip for *Lied im Schutt*; Meckel for *Ballade, Die Beute, Goldfisch*; Scharpenberg for *Ortsveränderung, Vergebens*.

Certain of the translations in this volume have been published previously by the following magazines. Grateful acknowledgments are given to *Atlas* for 5 poems; to *The Beloit Poetry Journal* for 3 poems; to *The Literary Review* for 1 poem; to *New Mexico Quarterly* for 1 poem; to *Approach* for 1 poem.

The translations of Brecht quoted by Professor Lange in his introduction are by John Willett, from his book *The Theatre of Bertolt Brecht*, New Directions; 1959.

INTRODUCTION

by VICTOR LANGE

At a time when the purposes and forms of art tend to become ever more universal, it is well to remember that works of the imagination always spring from the specific impulses of place and time, and that their roots are in our day as deeply imbedded in a local community of experience as they were in ages more obviously provincial than ours. No doubt, the history of modern poetry cannot be written in narrowly national terms: it is an involved and interdependent series of variations on themes common to us all; but it is not often that a significant contemporary poet can be truly effective without recognizing that he is bound in strength to the resources coming to him from a distinct tradition of feeling and form. Indeed, can we define and comprehend the voice of the English, American, French, or Italian poets of this age, however profoundly or appealingly each may transcend his special national assumptions, without listening very carefully to the resonances of a particular history and a particular speech? In the context of our contemporary view of poetry, are those peculiar national presuppositions—without which we cannot fully appreciate the European poets of the early nineteenth century—merely parochial predilections that have little importance within that overwhelming revolution of thinking and perception in which we all share?

Contemporary German poetry, of which the following pages will provide a comprehensive view, reflects, of course, the all-pervasive concerns of modern literature everywhere; its themes, like those of many French or American poets, are the sense of grief and apprehension with which the thinking and feeling human being must record the loss of certainty, his awareness of the efforts that he must make toward a comprehension of his disjointed world, and the conclusions, modest and tentative though they be, that may be drawn from his reflections. This complex of disquieting insight, assessment, and resolution is today the burden of poetry everywhere.

Yet, recent German poetry reflects this common mood in a manner strikingly consistent with its own history. For several generations German literature has been the mirror of a society that achieved its precarious coherence less than a century ago and that has remained stubbornly attached to jealousies of region and class that even two ravaging wars have not been able to extinguish. An incomparably energetic nation has been relentlessly concerned with its competitive opportunities, its achievements as well as its failures, while the poets and the thinkers, remarkable in their seriousness and ingenuity, have all too often stood aside, sometimes as purveyors of melancholy lyricism, more often in opposition and protest. As flashes of greatness and disastrous defeat have alternated in the course of German history, so the poet has played his role as Orpheus or Laocoön, sounding the voice of exhortation or of doom. The doer and the sayer have in Germany seldom coincided: from Nietzsche to Benn, from Hauptmann to Brecht, and from Thomas and Heinrich Mann to Böll or Grass, the German writer has acted as a skeptical and often militant critic of the aspirations of his society. "The true poet," says Heinz Piontek, one of the most articulate among the younger Germans, "must not march with his age, but fight it."

It may therefore seem paradoxical that the German poet occupies a peculiarly venerable place in the hierarchy of his culture; but if he accepts this traditional respect for the man of letters, he does so with that sharp awareness of isolation and irrelevance that Thomas Mann has so movingly represented. Unable to share with confidence in the convictions of the society that sustains him, he has often been inclined to escape into an imaginative counterworld of his own making. It is this paradox that has in Germany cast the poet in a more peremptory role than he is permitted to play elsewhere: Schiller's view of the artist as the most impressive coincidence of all human capacities is nowhere else asserted with equal fervor, and the poet who may, in this spirit, lay claim to being the conscience of his age, is the true maker of images of order and meaning. The German poet has tended, therefore, to embrace an attitude that is detached and experimental to the point of mannered eccentricity, and he has at times forced his intellectual or emotional irony to a degree where he can no longer count on being understood. No wonder that German literature seems often to take place in isolation from the community that is its subject matter.

2

Private lyricism, a reflective and probing intelligence, and an ironic sensibility skeptical of all social conventions—these have for long been the contradictory but powerful impulses of German poetry: Goethe and Hölderlin, Heine, Conrad Ferdinand Meyer, Rilke, Benn, and Brecht are among the most characteristic representatives. Although this tradition has often displayed national idiosyncrasies that appear at times to have divorced the German poets from the main stream of European poetry, during the past fifty years its intellectual presuppositions have become widely shared. To speak of the German and Austrian contribution to modern art—literature as well as painting, sculpture, and music—is to acknowledge a most influential body of perception and creativity in our time. Rilke and Brecht, as much as Kokoschka, Kandinsky, and Klee, Schönberg, Webern, and Berg, have shaped the language of contemporary feeling: their vision of a disintegrating system of values, which became first so overwhelmingly apparent within the social systems of Central Europe, has provided us with the terms of a universal experience.

In the great narrative experiments of the twenties and thirties—in Kafka, Musil, and Broch—the shock of this vast revolution of judgment has been registered with incomparable precision, and the history of more recent fiction suggests that the formal inventions of these novelists are still far from obsolete or exhausted. Thomas Mann may well have been right when, in 1936, he insisted that the novel with its "critical consciousness, the wealth of its devices, its free interplay of invention and reporting, musicality and cognition, myth and science, its human breadth, its objectivity and irony, is the representative and pre-eminently literary art-form of our time." But he must have spoken more in self-justification than in critical impartiality when he added that, compared to the modern novel, poetry and the drama are but archaic forms.

It is, in fact, not in the novel but in poetry that the imaginative energies of the past thirty years have found their most interesting expression: the poets rather than the novelists have emancipated themselves from the example of past masters; their work, whether American or European, is incomparably lively and serious. Poetry everywhere has reflected most intensely and most unambiguously the condition of our time. It has come to ask the ever present but ever more disturbing question as to the nature of reality within which we must find our way.

3

In Germany, certainly, lyric poetry offers the only substantial and coherent artistic accomplishment after the Second World War. Before we turn to examine this achievement more closely, it is well to remember the conditions that brought it about. Although the political collapse in 1945 has sometimes been compared to the events at the end of the First World War, beyond the harsh experience of national ruin, there is, in fact, little that the two periods have in common. In 1918 the established system of values crumbled, not merely as the result of defeat in war but because of long-prepared and persistent attacks from within—attacks that reflected the most articulate opposition and the most radical revolutionary thinking. In art as well as in politics, constant demands for fresh perspectives had prepared the challenging mood of the early twenties. A remarkably vocal resistance to bourgeois forms of life maintained itself, however precariously, for more than a decade, until it was effectively destroyed by the National Socialist regime. When this, in turn, was overthrown, it fell not because of any effective revolutionary forces within, but under the crushing onslaught of a victorious enemy. If 1945 offered to the Germans anything like a second chance of revolution, it was a chance altogether unprepared for and certainly lacking in that optimistic and humanitarian fervor of the years before and after 1918. A period of isolation and the sense of immense physical destruction and spiritual desolation compelled the Germans above all to survey what was left, what had happened outside, and what might be done toward recovery. These were pressing concerns, but they were not revolutionary challenges.

It would have been difficult at that time to predict the course of German letters. Only the most foolish observers could have expected an underground literature to emerge. That far-reaching outburst of experimental poetry between the wars, with its violent desire for emancipation from tradition, had long before come to an end, and its liberal representatives had, during the National Socialist era, been suppressed or driven into exile. The uncompromising and highly significant disavowal in the Dada movement of all aesthetic conventions, and the concern, in Cubism and Surrealism, with the constructive and metaphysical requirements of a new art, were in the era of Hitler only discredited memories of dangerous aberrations. Within Germany itself the years between 1930 and 1945 did not produce, either in fiction or in the drama, many works of more than ephemeral importance.

Lyrical poetry remained on the whole remarkably aloof from the political pressures toward social realism and simple-minded pathos. Distinguished poets such as Rudolf Alexander Schröder, Oskar Loerke, and Wilhelm Lehmann continued, cautiously and of course without the response of an adequate audience, to develop the manner of the great Magi of modern German poetry: George, Hofmannsthal, and Rilke.

Even after 1945 their stature has remained unquestioned; but their relevance to contemporary poetry has not been impressive. They were undoubtedly the most European among modern German poets: each of them was extraordinarily preoccupied with the role of the German writer within the traditions of European judgment and taste, and with his creative role in the present all-pervasive crisis of values. Like all symbolists they regarded the pursuit of art as a supreme form of human discipline. George's hopes, especially, of restoring the exemplary function of the poet as a moral preceptor in a disintegrating culture demanded a degree of formal austerity that is today no longer plausible or appealing. His view of poetry as a ritualistic and hieratic exercise is altogether discredited: the vision of greatness upon which his work rested can hardly be compelling to a generation skeptical of all large postulates.

Hofmannsthal's relatively small body of poetry, on the other hand, is now seen as similar in its essential purposes and its formal issues to the poetry of Yeats and Eliot, and its self-conscious attachment to the imaginative and social values and forms of his native Austrian tradition is recognized as symptomatic of the conservative concerns of a whole generation of European writers. Hofmannsthal would not have exercised so great an influence upon subsequent poets, if his mature work, his plays as well as his critical prose, had not deliberately subjected an early fascination with aestheticism to the insistent question as to the effectiveness of poetic speech in an age paralyzed by an awareness of its own complexity and ambiguity. Unlike Pound or Eliot, neither George nor Hofmannsthal was in a specific sense sufficiently interested in extending the formal devices of poetry to be of direct consequence to the younger German poets; however clear their understanding of the conditions of modern poetry, George's as well as Hofmannsthal's purpose was essentially restorative.

It was Rilke who moved most impressively toward an idiom representative of the modern disquiet over the discrepancy between an immensely rarefied intellectual sensibility, and the evanescent and elusive reality that is its object. The "reality" that Rilke wished to represent, he could no longer grasp as an object, whether disjointed or coherent: it became for him the very process of perception, the act, as it were, of encircling disparate aspects of experience from which a realm of tentative meaning might be constructed. Reality, this is to say, ceased to be an objective structure of meaning to be presupposed; it is henceforth for the poet the condition of experience to be made palpable in the poem itself: "I am writing poems," Günter Eich said not long ago, "to find my way in reality." Neither Rilke's intellectual mysticism nor his verbal mannerism were therefore of as much consequence to subsequent writers as his conviction that the poet can create a community of experience only by transforming into translucent images the ingredients of a world that threatens to fall away in meaninglessness.

Rilke's poetry, particularly his *Duino Elegies* and his *Sonnets to Orpheus,* subtle, introspective, and esoteric, provided between 1930 and 1950 for most German poets the gestures of speech by which the precarious balance between reality and inwardness, so characteristic of German thinking, could be represented. We need only to look at a comprehensive anthology such as Holthusen and Kemp's *Ergriffenes Dasein* (1953) to be struck by the Rilkean melody, syntax, and imagery that prevails in many of the best writers.

4

After 1945 the chief impulses came to the younger German writers less from George and Hofmannsthal than from the rediscovery of those European poets who are awkwardly grouped together as Expressionists or Surrealists. To call Rilke an expressionistic poet might blur the meaning of a term that offers, in any case, little more than a convenient label for a most heterogeneous experience. But if we recognize as the impulse common to the Expressionist artists, a desire not to express a private vision of the surrounding world, but, on the contrary, to convey the *process* of comprehension by which the objective world is being explored and established, Rilke represents a key figure of the Expressionist movement.

The Expressionist's sensibility is at once analytical and ecstatic; and the apocalyptic visions of Heym and Trakl, their dark and violent colors and their profound sense of solitude and paralysis in a monstrously fascinating world, were bound to appeal to the German writers after 1945. At a moment of radical self-scrutiny and in the face of an unparalleled denial of purpose, George's or Hofmannsthal's efforts toward cultural synthesis were far less attractive. These poets—and some of the other venerable elders of modern German poetry—had assumed an immanent correspondence between actuality and its representation in poetic language. To Hermann Hesse or Schröder, perhaps less inventive and more traditional than their more severely symbolist contemporaries, the natural setting of life offers a sufficient analogy for a transcendent order. For the Expressionists and their recent successors, reality is an infinite postulate that is rendered in the act of inquiry and of performance. Art produces reality instead of merely reproducing it; it creates knowledge rather than making it palatable. "The artist," Paul Klee reflected, "knows a great deal; but he knows it only after he has created it."

Gottfried Benn, in many ways the most widely influential modern German poet, offers an elaborate and brilliant commentary upon these issues. His poetry is an attempt at transcending the inherently meaningless material of life and the progressively disintegrating consciousness of modern man, in fascinating formal images; throughout his work as poet and essayist he echoes Nietzsche's assertion that the pursuit of art must be considered the last metaphysical activity of European nihilism. The middle ground between power and art is chaos; and to bare and represent the elusive character of reality is the ultimate task of poetry.

Like much modern writing, Benn's work has the character of a monologue, but, however resigned, it is a monologue conducted without the hopeless sense of isolation that is so strident in Heym and Trakl or, indeed, more self-indulgent in many of the early German romantic poets. Benn accepts for the poet the role of self-sufficient voice; he has no desire to engage in argument, to assert, to question or to persuade; he is resigned as to the scope of his social function, and without the reassurance of any common idealistic faith, has accepted the dismaying conclusion that the imparting of meaning is no longer achieved by the give and take of discourse. His poem exists as a hermetic utterance that seeks or needs no justification beyond its own being, and that serves no avowed purpose. It is "without faith and without hope, addressed to no one." The content of Benn's "absolute poem" is not the fortuitous world of actuality, but the sensibility of the poet himself.

This is not to say that for Benn and his successors, the world of actuality ceases to have any relevance; it is the cause and object of meditation and offers the ingredients for a design of reflections. Like the modern painter, Benn organizes reality, he does not represent it; like contemporary paintings, his poems are not produced at the moment of experience, not done, as it were, from nature; they are still lifes distilled and assembled in the study or the studio. If they contain emotion recollected in tranquillity, the act of recollection is far removed from the incidents of feeling. "The desk or the window seat develops more substance than the landscape itself; they give meaning to it, and transcend its irrelevancies and its indistinct seasonal character."

Benn's often asserted purpose is the attempt to neutralize "nature" in an act of inventive mastery and calculated reorganization that can only be performed in the work of art. Poetry rather than history, and art rather than any synthesizing philosophy, are the consummate achievements of man —not wars but artistic styles identify the great periods of civilization. What remains in the flux of experience is the "dream of form," the world as "spiritual construct," existence transposed into images.

Benn is entirely preoccupied with the synthetic capacities of the poetic process, that is to say, with the possibilities of finding compelling forms of speech by which the poetic intelligence can preserve itself alert and detached as a recorder of detailed and fragmented images. Verses such as "Verlorenes Ich" or "Fragmente" or "Du übersiehst dich nicht mehr...," familiar to any reader of modern German poetry, have the characteristic rhythm of Benn's own flat and melancholy voice, and their apparently casual movement deceives us as to the care and precision with which they have been put together. Once again, as in the seventeenth century, the poet claims not merely to make verses but to make sense. By his own admission, Benn's intention is similar to that of a scientist: his business is with composition rather than with any philosophy of feeling. "The lyrical poet moves about in a laboratory of words. There he models, manufactures words, opens them, explodes them, smashes them, in order to charge them with tensions that will continue for several decades. To make sentences, to find expressions, to be an artist, to work coolly and alone, not to speak to a community..."

It is, perhaps, not surprising that views at once so elegiac and so austere should have proved extraordinarily fascinating to many of the recent German poets. Benn's denial of all political and social concerns and, perhaps even more challenging, his refusal to permit the surrogate of speculation, whether religious or secular, to deflect the poet from his task of crystallizing reality in the work of art—this attitude, rather than any formal manner, has given Benn incomparable standing. His aestheticism has been taken not as a lyrical subterfuge and as means of escape, but as an imaginative procedure by which knowledge of self and of the world may be gained, probed, and preserved. For Benn, the aesthetic attitude is the truly appropriate mode of our time.

5

If Benn's poetry indicates an extreme resistance to individual involvement in the vagaries of history, it is Bertolt Brecht's overriding purpose to create, through poetry, a state of mind that leads to a reassessment of the judgments by which men determine their lives. Benn's conviction that the world is an essentially static phenomenon is in Brecht's work countered by a quasi-Marxist faith in the dynamic efficacy of reason and resolution. Brecht's work is directed not at mere detached recording of human inadequacy but toward revolutionary action.

The private and reserved monologue of Benn is in Brecht's theatrical writings and in his plain set poetry, superseded by an effort often in shrill and dissonant speech, to show, to demonstrate, and to teach. "To learn how to show what I see" —this is Brecht's intention as poet and dramatist:

> "How they step into each other's rooms with schemes
> Or rubber truncheons, or with cash
> How they stand in the streets and wait

How they lay traps for one another
Full of hope
How they make appointments
How they fasten on each other
How they make love
How they safeguard the loot
How they eat.
I show all that."

[From "The Playwright's Song" (1935).
Translated by John Willett]

Didactic poetry, long since discredited as a poetic form, has
in Brecht taken on fresh meaning: the clear-cut antithesis
between a rational, humane socialism and the deceptively
noble vocabulary by which irrational power often makes
itself palatable, produces poetry of remarkably direct strength;
unspecific as it is in its commitment to a Marxian philosophy, Brecht's seemingly straightforward but often slyly paro-
distic writing has offered the most plausible alternative to
the esoteric aloofness of Benn.

Brecht's language, it has been said by one critic, "can be
felt on the tongue, on the palate, in one's ears, in one's spine.
It is brutally sensuous, melancholy and tender. It contains
malice and bottomless sadness, grim wit and plaintive lyricism." But his aim as a poet has always been to explore, and
to persuade rather than merely to elaborate intellectual
alternatives. In his way he has, no less than any of his more
speculative contemporaries, been concerned with the efficacy of language, and with the manner of using it in a specific social context. This is to say that Brecht's poetry cannot
be divorced from his political convictions: for the first time
in the tradition of German "social" or "political" literature, a
firmly held—though never doctrinaire—ideological faith closely determines the structure of poetic forms. One of Brecht's
favorite forms is the ballad whose episodic twist and unem-
barrassed use of class-language he owes to Kipling; his Lied-

like compositions have almost nothing in common with the German romantic lyric; and by his witty chansons he seeks to hold the interest of a sophisticated night club audience or win the response of a shouting crowd of demonstrators.

But Brecht is not always caustic and aggressive; some of his poetry has a delicacy of line that is the result of far more than mere technical inventiveness: "The Lovers" is the most accomplished of these almost calligraphic pieces:

> See those wild cranes in a great circle sweeping!
> The clouds that lie behind them, soft and gentle
> Began to drift with them as they were leaving
> Their old life for another. Thus they went, all
> At the same height and with the same haste soaring
> Both of them seeming merely incidental.
> That cloudbank and wild bird should thus fly sharing
> The lovely sky which they so swiftly cover
> That neither therefore lingers in this clearing
> And neither sees a thing except how wavers
> The other in the wind which both feel brush them
> Who now in flight lie alongside each other.
> So into nothingness the wind may thrust them
> If neither of them alters or disperses
> So long will nothing have the power to touch them
> So long can they be chased away from all those places
> Where storms are threatening or shots re-echo.
> So under sun and moon's but slightly differing faces
> They fly away, each merging in his fellow.
> Where to? —Nowhere. Whom fleeing? —All of you.

[Translated by John Willett]

Unlike Trakl or Benn (or still more drastically Joyce or Pound) Brecht has never been interested in appraising and reorganizing the elementary particles of language; he has, rather, drawn deliberately upon the gestures of public speech. But instead of employing these gestures naïvely, naturalistically, or with lyrical or heroic pathos, he has brought to bear upon them skepticism and an ironic feeling for discredited cultural connotations. He has been suspicious of Schiller's peremptory posture and, especially, of what he felt to be Goethe's bland equivocations. By placing classical verse forms in a satirical context, he has in an unexpected way reinforced the uses of parody that form such an indispensable element in all modern analytical writing. Like Wedekind and Morgenstern, his direct German predecessors in the art of deliberately absurd understatement, Brecht has employed the clichés of speech in order to expose the clichés of experience; he has used "poetic" speech, shot through with elements of persiflage and parody ("auf die Poesie verzichten um die Poesie zu gewinnen"), as a means not merely of intellectual clarification, but of marshaling human energy through poetry within a distinctly postulated social frame.

With few exceptions, the language of German poetry had been elevated and divorced from ordinary speech. Brecht's use of an everyday vocabulary, of slang and platitudinous slogans, and of the casual manner of popular talk has immeasurably enriched the resources of contemporary German writing. The poem that so movingly introduces this anthology shows his mastery of the devices by which he hoped to make poetry simple and effective; it has become a model for all those younger German poets who have sought a way of breaking out of the paralyzing circle within which the single theme of ambiguity is all too often reiterated.

6

George, Hofmannsthal, Rilke, Benn, and Brecht—these five are above all others the great makers of modern German poetry: their influence, long after their death, cannot be missed—even where it is negative and indirect. Their inventions have enormously enlarged the vocabulary and intensified the speech of their successors. Neither Hermann Hesse nor Schröder, two older poets who died recently—both impressive and admirable writers, the one more romantic, the other classicist in temperament—suggest in their work the severely modern preoccupation with radical and experimental forms of speech. Like nearly all other major European poets of our time, they were concerned with the language of poetry either as the linguistic equivalent of an accepted reality, or as a means of creating reality. It is this distinction that enables us to speak, without being in any sense derogatory, of Hesse, Schröder, Agnes Miegel, and, among the younger poets, Rudolf Hagelstange, Albrecht Goes, or Friedrich Georg Jünger as "conventional" poets: they need not be trivial in their subject matter, but they are traditional in their belief in poetry as representation and prescription.

Like Robert Frost, these writers are essentially sustained by solid faith in the emotional, social, or religious energies of the individual, a conviction that enables them to postulate and proclaim a coherent and often transcendental order. Their belief in an inherently meaningful reality is reflected in traditional and disciplined poetic forms: where echoes of Goethe or Klopstock, Mörike or Platen are heard, where rhythmic patterns such as the hexameter or the Alcaic strophe are employed, where the sonnet or the ode offers formal stability, we recognize that the continuity of European culture, its secular or its religious tenets, is deliberately affirmed. The range in quality among these more traditional poets is, of course, considerable: we must decide whether a popular series of sonnets is more than a dubious effort to dress commonplace sentiments—however "modern"—in appealing poetic clichés, or whether the cyclical breadth of Schröder and the magnificent craftsmanship of Marie Luise Kaschnitz are not an entirely appropriate idiom for the anxiety, both profound and intelligent, felt at the ever-widening gulf between the perennial and the ephemeral energies of our particular contemporary perceptions.

For many of the poets in this anthology the adherence to conventional German speech and to the manner of their nineteenth-century predecessors such as Hölderlin or Droste-Hülshoff or Meyer is as natural as it is for others to accept the example of the three greatest European works of the past half century: Eliot's *Four Quartets*, Pound's *Cantos*, and Rilke's *Elegies*. In these the function of poetry is the rendering of the act of imagination and reflection. For these poets—as well as for Valéry, Wallace Stevens, Auden, Guillén, or Benn—reality is not given and fixed, it is rather to be established, its structure is to be seen and felt as a system of imaginative possibilities: its values are to be achieved rather than presupposed. Max Frisch, the Swiss dramatist, has teasingly suggested this as the purpose of modern poetry when he says that "we cannot demonstrate the truth, we must invent it." The process of inventing truth is most elaborately performed in the language of poetry, and we must not be surprised if the younger poets are less intent on dealing, however splendidly or movingly, with certain common experiences, than on demonstrating the very procedures and methods that would lead to the "invention" of possible truths.

We have come to see that the contemporary writer is no longer content with telling stories, developing plots, or offering anecdotal commentaries on private issues: he is instead, in Proust's metaphor, the man who knows how to become a mirror. He must make explicit the capacities through which we may learn, literally, to come to terms with reality. Neither inspiration nor intelligence seems adequate for this purpose —"The poet may lose his mind," suggests Piontek, "but he must not lose his memory." Through memory and reflection, dream and vision, he explores experience; by their very indirection these states of mind permit him to employ less rigid perspectives and more fluid views of the topography of the space he confronts than any naturalistic perception. His vision is by necessity refracted—"like the reflections in a glass," Rilke said of Trakl's poems.

It has been this desire to explore the sources of the imagination, both private and collective, that has brought many of the younger German poets to a rediscovery of Surrealism and Dadaism. A sense of the poetic possibilities of associative and accidental impulses—"dérèglement de la logique jusqu'à l'absurde, l'usage de l'absurde jusqu'à la raison" (Eluard)—has led them to the dream as a self-contained world, and thus to a kind of poetry that deliberately reasserts the intellectual assumptions of the German romantic tradition. Nature has supplied these writers with the objective detail for mosaics of memory or dream in which they have sought to establish the "invented truth." The apostrophe of nature as a realm of meaning that transcends in a peculiarly fascinating manner the business of everyday living, is in German poetry a sufficiently familiar and recurring theme; and to extract from the observed incidents of natural life something like reassuring metaphysical coherence has often been the preoccupation of the German writer. But after Rilke's urgent appeal to produce in the poem a meaning beyond the "barely tellable" things of the world, it is not surprising that more recently a group of less intricately speculative poets should have demonstrated that the "naming" itself of natural objects, of birds, stones, and flowers can be an act of poetic evocation, conveying a truth somewhere between natural science and magic.

Oskar Loerke and Wilhelm Lehmann have given currency to this idiom, which many after them have freely imitated and elaborated. "Nature" is for these poets an inexhaustible arsenal of animals and plants, of images, fragrances, associations, and impressions that link the human being to a demonic nether world in which he sometimes willingly immerses himself and from which he can in any case seldom escape: salamanders, vultures, hedge sparrows, grasshoppers, yellowhammers, swallowwort, poplar blossoms, aconite, darnel, and pimpernel—an astounding assortment of creatures and botanical specimens that sometimes suggests a nature handbook rather than any immediacy of experience.

Elisabeth Langgässer, who died in 1950, gave to this play of nature symbols an often ecstatic religious extension. In the poetry of Wilhelm Lehmann and Georg Britting—both first published in the nineteen thirties— this feeling for the magic of nature is most brilliantly and most exactly conveyed. The tone of the one is sharp and brittle and tends toward the playful and decorative; Britting works in a more Bavarian mode: dramatic, splendid, and intensely rich in atmospheric color. During the past ten years Karl Krolow has further developed and at the same time simplified Lehmann's manner of drawing the precisely observed natural object into a mythical context.

The success of these German "nature" poets—the term is an ambiguous and misleading one—is due to their refusal to indulge either in bucolic genre sketches or in pseudo-metaphysical effusiveness. They are seldom deceived as to the intellectual distance of the modern poet from the idyllic song or the enthusiastic ode; for it is not its sentimentality but a high degree of deliberate artifice that characterizes the most interesting of this recent nature poetry. In an attempt to multiply and intensify its capacity for evoking meaning it has frequently endowed its imagery with heraldic or fairytale associations: halcyons, griffins, and dragons have become part of a synthetic landscape that mirrors, beyond all actuality, the processes of reflection and perception.

Thus to elaborate the elements of nature and to reassemble them in a disciplined design is, of course, a procedure common to much modern poetry; it corresponds to Cézanne's conviction that nature in its plain actuality is always abhorrent and that its ingredients must be reduced—or enhanced—to their true function as metaphors of feeling. The still life, "nature morte," is therefore, not only in painting but in poetry, a peculiarly appropriate and appealing motif.

At it best, contemporary German nature poetry whatever its metaphors is, for this reason and others, not straightforward or photographic but "abstract": it conveys a multidimensional view of the world that the human being must consider more as a projection than as a reliable chart. Nothing is more characteristic of the best poets in this anthology than their acceptance of a reflective—as against a prescriptive—role, and their refusal, therefore, to teach, admonish, or deplore. The poet is a solitary figure who will neither affirm—unless it be in an authoritarian Marxist context—nor profitably attack, but only illuminate the conditions, natural or cultural, of his life. It is characteristic of the younger German poets that, even when they speak, often in strident tones, of their distaste for the contemporary scene, and their distrust of all proffered forms of social harmony, they do so without self-importance, without pathos, and above all without the Utopian fervor of their Expressionist predecessors. The prevalent themes of suffering and persecution, of solitude and inhumanity would be monotonous indeed if they were not used, in the best poetry, as occasions for a careful and intelligent exploration of their spiritual context. Celan's celebrated "Fugue of Death," a poem of extraordinary power, clarity, and discipline, is of these elucidations of a horrifying contemporary state of mind perhaps the most moving. But whatever the immediate incidents of melancholy or inhumanity, they are for the younger poets a cause of self-questioning rather than anger or despair; and they are seldom matters, we must not forget, that bear the give-and-take of dialogue.

Indeed, it is often hardly possible to say that the poet, in the common sense of that term, *speaks* to an audience; he uses words as transparencies, his language is a grid through which he observes and contemplates the world. Celan's best collection of poems, and perhaps the most important German body of poetry written after the war, is significantly entitled *Sprachgitter*—an image that Jean Paul frequently used and that indicates at once an awareness of the intrinsic limitation of speech, and the hope and promise of transcending it in the particular configuration of the poem.

Poetry, this is to say, is for the poets after the war, an exercise of language at its most specific and its most critical: as its function is to be pre-eminently cognitive, the poet is bound to be intensely concerned with the character of the language in which this act of knowledge becomes palpable. To many of the poets in this anthology, poetry means, precisely, that procedure, or that method, by which language is arranged so as to convey a tentative and "experimental" view of life. Even—or especially—in translation it will be felt that the individual word carries an extraordinary weight. Yet, the word is not, as it was for the symbolist as well as the Expressionist writer, an evocative complex of sensuous radiance. It is now used with a fine feeling for its conceptual range. If Benn detected or felt in the English word *evermore* overtones of *moor* as well as *la mort,* he could conclude that "words are much more than communication and content: they are on the one hand spiritual, and they convey on the other the essential ambiguity of all natural objects."

This acceptance of the ambiguity of speech is for the contemporary German poet one of the most consequential conditions of his craft: it is his answer to that increasing specificity of a language that, in a technological age, reduces and neutralizes the multiplicity of possible alternative meanings. The more rigidly closed a system of language becomes as a result of social and technical standardization, the more compelling is the necessity for the poet to break out of it. He knows that blurred or intensely private speech will not awaken in the reader the critical sensibilities that may lead him to an awareness of the incongruities and discrepancies between the authentic and the spurious. At its most articulate, poetry in our time often leads through the bizarre, the grotesque, or the comic, to a perception of what the eighteenth century called the sublime.

There have been few German poets so sharply conscious of the profound insights that "absurd" speech can convey as Edward Lear or Lewis Carroll; but Morgenstern and Ringelnatz several decades ago, and Enzensberger, Günter Grass, Peter Gan, Helmut Heissenbüttel, and Meckel in our own day, brilliantly employ the "eccentric" use of words in surprising syntactical relationships in order to demonstrate beyond all convention or standardization their mastery over the mobile resources of language. Like their French contemporaries, writers such as Jacques Prévert, or Raymond Queneau, they recognize that when the order between subject, object, and language is seriously in jeopardy—as it seems to be today—poetry must create conceptual possibilities and in the tentative exercise of speech produce fresh contexts of meaning.

The remarkable interest in the efficacy of language is bound at times to lead the younger German poets to elevated and precious diction, at others to a deliberately direct and "nonpoetic" speech. The reminiscences of Hölderlin's language that we find in the poetry of Ingeborg Bachmann are as legitimate and appropriate as the Biblical tone and imagery of Paul Celan, Nelly Sachs, Gertrud Kolmar, or Alfred Gong. A striving for tightly telescoped figures of speech has, in turn, produced a fashion for the Rilkean genitive metaphor: "the hummingbird of joy," "the morning of treetops," "the curve of the distance"—these have become rhetorical stereotypes of much contemporary writing. It is perhaps more in keeping with the ironic temper of much modern poetry if Enzensberger, Meckel, or Grass write plainly but wittily and with a calculated sense for the disparity between the play of comic associations and the unspoken claims of common sense. This vividly contemporary speech is, of course, the chosen vehicle particularly of those poets who are intent, in however subtle a manner, on social criticism or, at any rate, on providing "usable poetry." Enzensberger, a writer of great versatility, wished his first volume of poetry, *Defense of the Wolves* (1957), to be taken as "slogans, posters, leaflets, scratched on a wall, stuck on a wall, handed out by a wall." His "angry" as well as his "friendly" or "melancholy" poems are incisive protests against moral and intellectual delusion and easy comfort. But however brittle and crackling Enzensberger's speech may be it is not so rarefied, nor indeed so skeletonized, as the language of such an extraordinarily self-conscious poet as Heissenbüttel. His poems spring from a peculiarly sharp feeling for the multiple resonance of words; they are carefully controlled attempts at creating "linguistic spaces," within which a circumscribed and "experimental" meaning arises. Heissenbüttel's *Combinations* and *Topographies* are sublime games that come closest to the notion of poetry as an exercise by which reality is in the poem not reproduced or reflected, but established. "Reality," he has said, in the spirit of Wittgenstein, "is for me only what can be formulated."

The organizing principle of much contemporary German poetry is its compelling rhythm, its syntactical design, and the structural concatenation of images; with few noticeable exceptions, rhyme and elaborate classical verse forms seem to have almost entirely disappeared as unifying or dramatic devices. Celan's "Death Fugue" is the model of a remarkable skill in plotting a straight and uninterrupted course of feeling, made increasingly intense and complex by the repetition and variation of a few images and key words, the breathless chant, the hammering insistence on staying with overwhelming and nightmarish memories of anguish and horror. In this poem the arc of suspense, both formal and intellectual, is perfectly maintained without rhyme or conventional versification. Even where these are still employed—most appropriately in the work of Kaschnitz, Krolow, or Piontek—they are subordinated to the compelling immediacy of the speaking voice, and to the coherence that is created by tightly interlocked metaphors and distinctly related perceptions.

The speech of the best of contemporary German poetry, whether it obeys the conventions of versification or whether it deliberately denies them, is in any case neither vague nor pretentious, neither flamboyant nor impulsive; it shuns slurring, and all inarticulate outbursts; every word must stand on its specific claims, no element of the language may be taken for granted. The accepted grammar of classical discourse has given way to forms of discontinuity or simultaneity and to the staccato effects of juxtaposition. To read these poems aloud, or to hear them spoken by the poets themselves, is to recognize the extraordinary scrutiny that each word has received, and to feel that "rage to order words" that gives fascination to so much modern writing.

Severity of rhythmic and syntactical effects and bareness of structure have in most of the new German poets replaced the large and ample solidity of an earlier manner. Yet, this interest in design is only a means to the end of a more concentrated application of intelligence and emotion to the specific incidents of life. Like the contemporary musician and painter, these poets tend to distill and crystallize images to the point of abstraction. And abstraction is too often only another term for obscurity. But obscure the modern poet cannot allow himself to be, even though what he has to say may refer to unfamiliar perspectives of a world that outwardly seems familiar. He has every right to protest that the language of the modern physicist is incomparably more obscure than his own. In a strange and abrupt poem entitled "Lost Identity," Gottfried Benn refers to the devastating consequences of our inquiries into a universe that has been, as he puts it, "thought to pieces" by turning "space and time and what wove and weighed mankind" into a mere "function of eternities." This process of infinite elucidation— "where do you end, where do you camp, where do your spheres extend?"—may now be rendered most intelligibly by the poetic act.

7

In Germany and elsewhere, poetry seems no longer to provide comfort or reassurance; it unsettles, and haunts and stirs the imagination of the reader; it tests the common formulas of speech or feeling against an awareness of the insecurity and precariousness of life and judgment. To this skeptical mood, the experiences of the recent past, whether horrendous or grotesque or merely puzzling, have, of course, contributed; but neither the war nor the recollections of the Hitler decade and the confusion of its aftermath provide as such the topics of these poems. For most of the younger poets these events are only symbols of a historical situation in which the self is peculiarly determined by the universal, in which love poetry and public poetry stem from the same hopes and fears, and in which little solace can be derived from any idealism or from the contemplation of a presumed natural order. It is only in the work of some of the East German poets that ideological postulates have achieved a poetry of direct political purpose: the official poet laureate Kurt Bartels (Kuba), Erich Weinert, S. Hermlin, or Arnim Müller are committed to a socialist and antibourgeois art in which the objectives and the forms of writing are dictated by a revolutionary faith. There are others in the East—Louis Fürnberg, Georg Maurer, Erich Arendt, or Günter Deicke—who have in their often moving poetry transcended the narrow vocabulary of exhortatory pathos. Strangely enough, none of these poets has learned from Bertolt Brecht: their masters, whether they are disguised or modified, are Hölderlin, Trakl, and Rilke. Peter Huchel, one of the two Eastern poets who appear in this anthology, belongs in his most distinguished work to that group of nature-symbolists for whom, in the West, Loerke is the decisive model and among whom today Lehmann and Krolow are the best known.

Among the Western poets, the coincidence between private emotion and disciplined public commitment is seldom an explicit aim. The idea of community, so widely put in question and discredited by recent history, remains less a postulate than a vision. Not many poets assert—like Goes or Hagelstange—their faith in the consoling and continuing strength of a sustaining European culture. The persistent image of the human being haunted by fear and the recollection of horror and destruction, is forever placed in new dimensions of insight and compassion: grief and lament, the solitude of a bitter and silent heart, the displaced, dispossessed, and disoriented, the division by frontiers of mind and feeling, the scattered body of defeated believers, man between freedom and ruthless power, dark memories and the certainty only of darker days to come—these are the themes of most of the poems that express an attitude at once deeply moved and willing to accept the condition of insecurity.

Time, that great reminder of perpetual crisis, again and again receives in this poetry its transparent definition. Celan, as well as Bachmann, relates all human experience to its chimerical ambiguity: it is past and future, barely apprehended in a self-destroying present, felt only in its transitoriness and as a reminder of death. Holthusen's superb "Variations on Time and Death" and Krolow's "Poems against Death" attempt to maintain a view of life that receives its affirmation in the awareness of the insubstantiality of self.

The world of objects and of sensuality is felt all the more intensely, since it is perceived—to use a Nietzschean metaphor—"as strange to us and not our own, as a power next to our power." If for Rilke the poets were the "bees of the invisible," it is now the absolute assertion of the "visible" over any speculative synthesis that challenges the poet. Many of the younger German poets have read Donne and the English metaphysical poets: like them they are concerned with the baffling and terrifying relationship between the temporal and the ineffable; and in their work, too, transcendence is achieved by a tightly woven pattern of physical images surprisingly joined and contrasted.

It is not sentimentality when the heart is over and again evoked as the chief source of community as well as cognition; for love and knowledge, either in their secular or their religious motivation, are the interdependent energies of understanding. Ingeborg Bachmann's poem "Explain it, love," and Holthusen's "What is love when it comes to pass in this time" are characteristic and scrupulous explorations of the range within which the poet may today speak of the modes and the efficacy of love. In either case, love is the medium of a *religious* experience that is evoked not so much to comprehend as to bear the paradoxical presence, so inescapably witnessed by all who survived the war, of destruction and salvation, and of despair and illumination. In Alfred Gong's poem "Cognition" the image of the Saviour is recast after the holocaust, "of ashes, of brimstone, of tears, of heart and heart and heart."

8

It will be readily seen that the poets whose work is represented in this anthology are remarkably varied in their attitudes toward private or social concerns, and that they differ to an extraordinary degree in their views of the form and function of poetry. They cannot be classified by any single "ism"; they show no group coherence, and they acknowledge few masters. They may have learned from Benn and Brecht within the German tradition, or from Valéry and Pound, those formidable European examples of a disciplined, self-conscious, and highly figurative poetry. If some of them appear conventional in attitude or form, they are not commonplace in their convictions but rather choose to submit to the demanding responsibilities of tradition. If others are aggressively impatient of continuity and maintain that self-assertive and eccentric manner so characteristic of German poetry as a whole, they reflect a desire for an idiom that is unmistakably in keeping with the introspective and analytical nature of contemporary writing everywhere. None of these poets is, at any rate, content with the easy flow of lyrical mood or with pleasing paraphrase. On the contrary, they are intensely preoccupied with the *means* of saying, as much as with subject matter, and they are still more concerned with the resources of language and rhythm, with the compressed and complex image, than with the deceptive shortcuts of convivial discourse. Nor do they always feel able to offer the palpable whole of an event or a feeling, but they lay bare and explore its components, its ambience, and its momentary bearing upon a vision of truth.

However uncertain this vision of truth may be, its "provenance," in the meaning of Günter Eich's poem, is lucidly pursued, and its facets are patiently caught in poetic statements that are as cautious as they wish to be reliable. If truth can no longer be readily seen as an unequivocal substance, it is, nevertheless, apprehended as a presence to be constantly faced and recognized in those "signs of the world" that are evoked in many of these poems. Poetry, this is to say, is here pursued as an act of self-comprehension and of self-definition, undertaken without illusions and conveyed in turn without pathos or laziness of mind or language.

To have these poems before us in their original language, as well as in the mirror, as it were, of a sensitive English translation, will sharpen our perception of their special intentions. There is no need to argue the plausible and, alas, fashionable platitude that poetry cannot be translated. It is as true as any platitude; but we should be foolish to take it as the whole truth. Poetry is not merely design and syntax, but a web of images that reveals to us a whole system of feeling and insight. At its most conscientious best, a translation will manage to reproduce much of the experience that has become crystallized in the original gestures of poetic speech—not all, of course, but enough to make us regret our ignorance of the original and of the precision and the singular efficacy of the poet's own language. For in the poetry of our time, whether English, German, or French, this sort of exactitude is the supreme virtue: we value sparseness rather than a vaguely enveloping emotion; we respect the clarity of judgment that illuminates the imagination; and we prefer concentric circles of meaning to overwhelming waves of effusion and sentiment.

V. L.

An Anthology of Contemporary German Poetry

Bertolt Brecht

AN DIE NACHGEBORENEN

I

Wirklich, ich lebe in finsteren Zeiten!
Das arglose Wort ist töricht. Eine glatte Stirn
Deutet auf Unempfindlichkeit hin. Der Lachende
Hat die furchtbare Nachricht
Nur noch nicht empfangen.

Was sind das für Zeiten, wo
Ein Gespräch über Bäume fast ein Verbrechen ist
Weil es ein Schweigen über so viele Untaten einschließt!
Der dort ruhig über die Straße geht
Ist wohl nicht mehr erreichbar für seine Freunde
Die in Not sind?

Es ist wahr: ich verdiene noch meinen Unterhalt
Aber glaubt mir: das ist nur ein Zufall. Nichts
Von dem, was ich tue, berechtigt mich dazu, mich
        sattzuessen.
Zufällig bin ich verschont. (Wenn mein Glück aussetzt
Bin ich verloren.)

Man sagt mir: iß und trink du! Sei froh, daß du hast!
Aber wie kann ich essen und trinken, wenn
Ich es dem Hungernden entreiße, was ich esse, und
Mein Glas Wasser einem Verdurstenden fehlt?
Und doch esse und trinke ich.

Ich wäre gerne weise.
In den alten Büchern steht, was weise ist:
Sich aus dem Streit der Welt halten und die kurze Zeit

Bertolt Brecht

TO POSTERITY 33¾

I

Really, I live in evil times!
A guileless word is foolish. A smooth brow
Hints at indifference. He who still can laugh
Has not yet received
The terrible news.

What times are these when
It is almost a crime to talk of trees
For that means silence about so many evil deeds!
Maybe he who quietly crosses the street
Is out of reach now for his friends
Who are in danger?

It is true: I am still making a living
But, believe me, that is only luck. Nothing
Of all I do entitles me to eat my fill.
By chance I was spared. (If my luck leaves me
I am lost.)

They tell me: eat and drink! Be glad you have it!
But how can I eat and drink
When I snatch from the hungry what I eat,
And my glass of water is taken from the thirsty?
Yet I eat and drink.

I would love to be wise.
It is set down in the old books what wisdom is:
To keep away from the strife of the world

Ohne Furcht verbringen
Auch ohne Gewalt auskommen
Böses mit Gutem vergelten
Seine Wünsche nicht erfüllen, sondern vergessen
Gilt für weise.
Alles das kann ich nicht:
Wahrlich, ich lebe in finsteren Zeiten!

2

In die Städte kam ich zu der Zeit der Unordnung
Als da Hunger herrschte.
Unter die Menschen kam ich zu der Zeit des Aufruhrs
Und ich empörte mich mit ihnen.
So verging meine Zeit
Die auf Erden mir gegeben war.

Mein Essen aß ich zwischen den Schlachten.
Schlafen legte ich mich unter die Mörder.
Der Liebe pflegte ich achtlos
Und die Natur sah ich ohne Geduld.
So verging meine Zeit
Die auf Erden mir gegeben war.

Die Straßen führten in den Sumpf zu meiner Zeit.
Die Sprache verriet mich dem Schlächter.
Ich vermochte nur wenig. Aber die Herrschenden
Saßen ohne mich sicherer, das hoffte ich.
So verging meine Zeit
Die auf Erden mir gegeben war.

Die Kräfte waren gering. Das Ziel
Lag in großer Ferne,
Es war deutlich sichtbar, wenn auch für mich
Kaum zu erreichen.
So verging meine Zeit
Die auf Erden mir gegeben war.

And to live your short time without fear,
Also to avoid violence,
To return good for evil,
Not to fulfill one's wishes but to forget them,
That is supposed to be wise.
All that I cannot do:
Really, I live in evil times!

2

I came to the cities in a time of unrest
When hunger reigned.
In a time of rebellion, I came to the people
And I rebelled with them.
Thus I spent the time
That was given to me on earth.

I ate my food between battles.
I laid me down to sleep among murderers.
Heedlessly I loved
And impatiently I looked upon nature.
Thus I spent the time
That was given to me on earth.

Roads led only into bogs in my day.
My speech betrayed me to the slaughterer.
There was little I could do. But without me
The rulers sat more secure, or so I hoped.
Thus I spent the time
That was given to me on earth.

Men's strength was limited. The goal
Lay in the far future,
I could see it distinctly but it was
Barely in reach for me.
Thus I spent the time
That was given to me on earth.

3

Ihr, die ihr auftauchen werdet aus der Flut
In der wir untergegangen sind,
Gedenkt
Wenn ihr von unseren Schwächen sprecht
Auch der finsteren Zeit
Der ihr entronnen seid.

Gingen wir doch, öfter als die Schuhe die Länder wechselnd
Durch die Kriege der Klassen, verzweifelt
Wenn da nur Unrecht war und keine Empörung.

Dabei wissen wir ja:
Auch der Haß gegen die Niedrigkeit
Verzerrt die Züge.
Auch der Zorn über das Unrecht
Macht die Stimme heiser. Ach, wir
Die wir den Boden bereiten wollten für Freundlichkeit
Konnten selber nicht freundlich sein.

Ihr aber, wenn es so weit sein wird
Daß der Mensch dem Mensch ein Helfer ist,
Gedenkt unsrer
Mit Nachsicht.

Rudolf Alexander Schröder

DIE BRÜCKE

Götter und Genien alle, des Reisenden fromme Geleiter,
Wahret—o laßt euch erflehn!—wahret das steinerne Joch,
Das in der gräßlichen Leere getrost, ein Wunder,
  hinauslehnt,
Schmal wie der Iris Bug, aber zu dauern bestimmt.

3

You, who will emerge from the flood
In which we perished,
Consider,
When you speak of our iniquities,
Consider the dark days
That you escaped.

For we lived, changing our countries more often
        than our shoes
Through a war of classes, despairing
When there was only injustice and no rebellion.

Yet this we know:
Even the hatred of baseness
Distorts the features.
Even wrath against wrong
Makes the voice harsh. Oh, even we
Who were to prepare the ground for kindliness—
We ourselves could not be kind.

But you, when it will come to pass
That man will be a helper of man,
Think of us
With compassion.

Rudolf Alexander Schröder

THE BRIDGE

Gods, and all genii, who are the traveler's pious companions,
Guard, we implore you, O gods, safeguard the yoke made
        of stone.
Trustingly it leans forward, thus defying the void,
Narrow like iris blossoms, yet it is meant to last.

Stürzt es, so stürzt in Hälften die Welt; zurück in sich selber
Flüchtet Entsetzen, es scheut selbst der Gedanke den Sprung.
Nur solang ihr sie fristet, die heilig Schwebende, tauschen,
Über der Brücke gesellt, Diesseits und Jenseits den Kuß.

Wilhelm Lehmann

AUF SOMMERLICHEM FRIEDHOF, (1944)

Der Fliegenschnäpper steinauf, steinab.
Der Rosenduft begräbt dein Grab.
Es könnte nirgends stiller sein:
Der darin liegt, erschein, erschein!

Der Eisenhut blitzt blaues Licht.
Komm, wisch den Schweiß mir vom Gesicht.
Der Tag ist süß und ladet ein,
Noch einmal säßen wir zu zwein.

Sirene heult, Geschützmaul bellt.
Sie morden sich: es ist die Welt.
Komm nicht! Komm nicht! Laß mich allein,
Der Erdentag lädt nicht mehr ein.
Ins Qualenlose flohest du,
O Grab, halt deine Tür fest zu!

If it should break, the world would split, and sink back
    to despair,
Even the mind then would dread to leap across the abyss.
Only as long as the gods will sustain the suspended, the holy,
Will the Here and the There, spanning the bridge,
    meet and kiss.

Wilhelm Lehmann

SUMMERY GRAVEYARD, (1944)

Flycatcher glides in sweeping wave,
Fragrance of roses buries your grave.
No stiller resting place than here:
You, who are sleeping beneath—Appear! Appear!

Aconite gleams in cold-blue blaze.
Come wipe the damp now from my face.
The day is sweet, asks you to come,
Once more we would be in the sun.

Sirens scream, cannons bark.
They murder each other: this is our world.
Don't come! Don't come! I'll stay alone!
Where you dwell suffering is not known.
Our earthly life invites no more,
O grave, keep closed your door.

Wilhelm Lehmann

OBERON

Durch den warmen Lehm geschnitten
Zieht der Weg. Inmitten
Wachsen Lolch und Bibernell.
Oberon ist ihn geritten,
Heuschreckschnell.

Oberon ist längst die Sagenzeit hinabgeglitten.
Nur ein Klirren
Wie von goldnen Reitgeschirren
Bleibt,
Wenn der Wind die Haferkörner reibt.

Gottfried Benn

VERLORENES ICH

Verlorenes Ich, zersprengt von Stratosphären,
Opfer des Ion—: Gamma-Strahlen-Lamm—
Teilchen und Feld—: Unendlichkeitschimären
auf deinem grauen Stein von Notre-Dame.

Die Tage gehn dir ohne Nacht und Morgen,
die Jahre halten ohne Schnee und Frucht
bedrohend das Unendliche verborgen—
die Welt als Flucht.

Wo endest du, wo lagerst du, wo breiten
sich deine Sphären an—Verlust, Gewinn—:
ein Spiel von Bestien: Ewigkeiten,
an ihren Gittern fliehst du hin.

Wilhelm Lehmann

OBERON

Cut into the warm red loam
A path is leading, overgrown
With pimpernel and beggar-tick.
Oberon was riding here,
Grasshopper-quick.

Oberon slips back to legendary times
But there remains a jingling
As from his golden
Spur
When in the wind the quivering grasses
Stir.

Gottfried Benn

LOST IDENTITY

Lost ego, split by stratospheres,
victim of ion—lamb of the gamma ray,
particle, also field: chimeras of infinity
on Notre Dame, stony and gray.

The years hold neither snow nor fruit,
your days are passing without dawn or night,
they hold infinity—a menace—hidden:
The world as flight.

Where do you end, where do you camp,
where do your spheres extend—
Loss, gain: a game for beasts. Eternities:
your flight across their bars will never end.

Der Bestienblick: die Sterne als Kaldaunen,
der Dschungeltod als Seins— und Schöpfungsgrund,
Mensch, Völkerschlachten, Katalaunen
hinab den Bestienschlund.

Die Welt zerdacht. Und Raum und Zeiten
und was die Menschheit wob und wog,
Funktion nur von Unendlichkeiten—
die Mythe log.

Woher, wohin—nicht Nacht, nicht Morgen,
kein Evoë, kein Requiem,
du möchtest dir ein Stichwort borgen—
allein bei wem?

Ach, als sich alle einer Mitte neigten
und auch die Denker nur den Gott gedacht,
sie sich den Hirten und dem Lamm verzweigten,
wenn aus dem Kelch das Blut sie rein gemacht,

und alle rannen aus der einen Wunde,
brachen das Brot, das jeglicher genoß—
oh ferne zwingende erfüllte Stunde,
die einst auch das verlorne Ich umschloß.

Gottfried Benn

EBERESCHEN

Ebereschen—noch nicht ganz rot
von jenem Farbton, wo sie sich entwickeln
zu Nachglut, Vogelbeere, Herbst und Tod.

Ebereschen—noch etwas fahl,
doch siehe schon zu einem Strauß gebunden

Death in the jungle: the reason for creation.
Glance of the beast: stars are entrails.
Man, Catalaunian Plains, and battles of the nations,
slide down the gullet of the beast.

World thought to pieces. Space, and time,
and that which mankind wove and weighed,
they are but functions of eternities.
Religions lied.

Where to, where from—not night not morning,
no evoe, no requiem,
what you need is a borrowed slogan—
borrowed from whom?

Oh, when they all bowed toward one single center,
when even the thinkers only thought: the God,
when they branched out to lamb and shepherds,
blood of the chalice had purified them,

then all flowed from one wound;
all broke the bread and ate it in serenity—
distant, compelling hour of fulfillment
that once enclosed our lost identity.

Gottfried Benn

MOUNTAIN ASH

Berries of mountain ash—just a shade less
than that red hue when they will turn
to afterglow—bird-berries, autumn, death.

Berries of mountain ash—not in their prime,
but look, already forming a bouquet,

ankündigend halbtief die Abschiedsstunden:
vielleicht nie mehr, vielleicht dies letzte Mal.

Ebereschen—dies Jahr und Jahre immerzu
in fahlen Tönen erst und dann in roten
gefärbt, gefüllt, gereift, zu Gott geboten—
wo aber fülltest, färbtest, reiftest du—?

Gottfried Benn

ACH, DAS FERNE LAND

Ach, das ferne Land,
wo das Herzzerreißende
auf runden Kiesel
oder Schilffläche libellenflüchtig
anmurmelt,
auch der Mond
verschlagenen Lichts
—halb Reif, halb Ährenweiß—
den Doppelgrund der Nacht
so tröstlich anhebt—

ach, das ferne Land,
wo vom Schimmer der Seen
die Hügel warm sind,
zum Beispiel Asolo, wo die Duse ruht,
von Pittsburg trug sie der „Duilio" heim,
alle Kriegsschiffe, auch die englischen, flaggten
        halbmast,
als er Gibraltar passierte—

dort Selbstgespräche
ohne Beziehungen auf Nahes,

half-deep proclaiming hours of parting-day:
perhaps no more, perhaps just this last time.

Berries of mountain ash—this year and always new,
palely at first, then in red glow,
tinted, filled, ripened, offered unto God—
but did you deepen and mature, but did you grow?

Gottfried Benn

OH, THE FAR LAND

Oh, the far land
where heartache
murmurs, dragon-fly-fleetingly
over round pebbles
or reed,
the moon, too,
with cunning light
—half hoarfrost, half grain-white—
so comfortingly points out
the double ground
of the night.

Oh, the far land,
where hills are warm
with the shimmering of lakes,
like Asolo where the Duse rests,
the "Duilio" carried her home from Pittsburgh,
all men-of-war, even the British, displayed their flags
        at half-mast
as she passed Gibraltar—

there monologues
without relation to the familiar,

Selbstgefühle
frühe Mechanismen,
Totemfragmente
in die weiche Luft—
etwas Rosinenbrot im Rock—

so fallen die Tage,
bis der Ast am Himmel steht,
auf dem die Vögel einruhn
nach langem Flug.

Gottfried Benn

ZERSTÖRUNGEN

Zerstörungen—
aber wo nichts mehr zu zerstören ist,
selbst die Trümmer altern
mit Wegerich und Zichorie
auf ihren Humusandeutungen,
verkrampft als Erde—

Zerstörungen—
das sagt immerhin: Hier war einmal
Masse, Gebautes, Festgefügtes—
o schönes Wort
voll Anklang
an Füllungsreichtum
und Heimatfluren—

Zerstörungen—
o graues Siebenschläferwort
mit Wolken, Schauern, Laubverdunkeltheiten,

egotism,
early mechanisms,
totem-fragments
in soft air—
a little raisin bread in the coat pocket—

thus sink the days,
until there is limned on the sky
the bough
where birds rest
after long flight.

Gottfried Benn

DESTRUCTION

Destruction—
but where there is nothing left to be destroyed
even rubble ages
with white mullein and chicory
on traces of humus,
convulsed as soil—

Destruction—
that means nevertheless: here was once
Massiveness, Design, Construction—
Oh, beautiful word
reminiscent of
full-blown riches
and fields at home—

Destruction—
Oh gray seven-sleeper word
with clouds, showers, darkened foliage

gesichert für lange Zeit—
wo Sommer sein sollte
mit Fruchtgetränken,
Eisbechern, beschlagenen,
und Partys zu heller Nacht am Strande.

Gottfried Benn

MENSCHEN GETROFFEN

Ich habe Menschen getroffen, die
wenn man sie nach ihrem Namen fragte,
schüchtern—als ob sie gar nicht beanspruchen könnten,
auch noch eine Benennung zu haben—
„Fräulein Christian" antworteten und dann:
„wie der Vorname", sie wollten einem die Erfassung
        erleichtern,
kein schwieriger Name wie „Popiol" oder
        „Babendererde"—
„wie der Vorname"—bitte, belasten Sie Ihr
        Erinnerungsvermögen nicht!

Ich habe Menschen getroffen, die
mit Eltern und vier Geschwistern in einer Stube
aufwuchsen, nachts, die Finger in den Ohren,
am Küchenherde lernten,
hochkamen, äußerlich schön und ladylike wie
        Gräfinnen—
und innerlich sanft und fleißig wie Nausikaa,
die reine Stirn der Engel trugen.

Ich habe mich oft gefragt und keine Antwort gefunden,
woher das Sanfte und das Gute kommt,
weiß es auch heute nicht und muß nun gehn.

sure to remain for a long time—
where it should be summer
with fruit drinks,
dewy ice-cream cups,
and beach parties in luminous night.

Gottfried Benn

PEOPLE MET

I met people who
if one were to ask their name
would answer modestly
"Miss James"—as if they dared not even
claim their own name—and then:
"like the first name,"—they wanted to make it easier for you,
not a difficult name like "Popiol" or
        "Babendererde"—
"like the first name,"—please, don't burden
        your memory.

I met people who
grew up in one room
with their parents and four brothers and sisters,
and who, nights, fingers in ears,
learned at the kitchen stove,
rose in the world—outwardly beautiful and ladylike
        as a countess—
inwardly gentle and diligent as Nausicaä, and
with the pure brow of angels.

I have often asked myself but found no answer:
where do gentleness and goodness come from.
I do not know, even today—and now I must go.

Hans Arp

DIE EBENE

Ich befand mich allein mit einem Stuhl auf einer Ebene,
  Die sich in einen leeren Horizont verlor.
  Die Ebene war fehlerlos asphaltiert.
  Nichts, aber auch gar nichts außer mir und
dem Stuhl befand sich auf ihr.
  Der Himmel war immerwährend blau.
  Keine Sonne belebte ihn.
  Ein unerklärliches, unvernünftiges Licht erhellte
die endlose Ebene.
  Wie künstlich aus einer anderen Sphäre projiziert,
  Erschien mir dieser ewige Tag.
  Ich hatte nie Schlaf, nie Hunger, nie Durst,
nie heiß, nie kalt.
  Da sich nichts auf dieser Ebene ereignete und veränderte,
  War die Zeit nur ein abwegiges Gespenst.
  Die Zeit lebte noch ein wenig in mir,
  Und dies hauptsächlich wegen des Stuhles.
  Durch meine Beschäftigung mit ihm verlor
ich den Sinn für Vergangenes nicht ganz.
  Ab und zu spannte ich mich, als sei ich ein
Pferd, vor den Stuhl
und trabte mit ihm bald im Kreis, bald geradeaus.
  Daß es gelang, nehme ich an,
  Ob es gelang, weiß ich nicht,
  Da sich ja im Raume nichts befand,
  An dem ich meine Bewegung hätte
nachprüfen können.
  Saß ich auf dem Stuhl, so grübelte ich traurig,
aber nicht verzweifelt,
  Warum das Innere der Welt ein solch schwarzes
Licht ausstrahlte.

Hans Arp

THE PLAIN

I was alone with a chair on a plain
     That lost itself in a void horizon.
     The plain was faultlessly asphalted.
     Nothing, absolutely nothing, but the chair and I
were on this plain.
     The sky was forever blue,
     No sun gave life to it.
     An inscrutable, insensible light illuminated
the infinite plain.
     To me this eternal day seemed to be projected
—artificially—from a different sphere.
     I was never sleepy nor hungry nor thirsty,
never hot nor cold.
     Time was only an abstruse ghost since nothing
happened or changed in this plain.
     In me Time still lived a little
     And this was mainly on account of the chair.
     Owing to my occupation with it I did not completely
lose my sense of the past.
     Now and then I would hitch myself, as if I were a horse,
to the chair
     and would trot around with it, sometimes in circles,
and sometimes straight ahead.
     I assume that I succeeded.
     Whether I really succeeded I do not know
     Since there was nothing in space
     By which I could have checked my movements.
     As I sat on the chair I pondered sadly, but not desperately,
     Why the core of the world exuded such black light.

Nelly Sachs

Aber vielleicht
haben wir
vor Irrtum Rauchende
doch ein wanderndes Weltall geschaffen
mit der Sprache des Atems?

Immer wieder die Fanfare
des Anfangs geblasen?
Das Sandkorn in Windeseile geprägt
bevor es wieder Licht ward
über der Geburtenknospe des Embryos?

Und sind immer wieder
eingekreist in Deinen Bezirken
auch wenn wir nicht der Nacht gedenken
und der Tiefe des Meeres
unsere Worte nur hinstellen
wie flache Teller mit Leere.

Und bestellen doch Deinen Acker
hinter dem Rücken des Todes?

Vielleicht sind die Umwege
des Sündenfalles
wie der Meteore heimliche Fahnenfluchten
doch im Alphabet der Gewitter
eingezeichnet neben den Regenbögen?

Wer weiß auch
die Grade des Fruchtbarmachens
und wie die Saaten gebogen werden
aus fortgezehrten Erdreichen
für die saugenden Münder des Lichts?

Nelly Sachs

BUT PERHAPS...

But perhaps
we
beclouded with errors
created a wandering world
with the speech of breath?

blew again and again
the fanfare of beginning?
coined a grain of sand with lightning speed
before there would be light again
upon the birth-bud of the embryo?

Trapped as we are again
and again in your circuit
even though we may not consider the night
and the depth of the sea
only placing our words
like shallow plates filled with emptiness.

Are we tilling your field
at the back of Death?

Perhaps the detours
of the fall of man
like secret desertion of meteors
are marked in the alphabet of thunderstorms
along with rainbows?

Who could ever know
the grades of fructification
and how seed is bent
in barren soil
toward the sucking lips of light?

Agnes Miegel

WAGEN AN WAGEN

Um Allerseelen
In der dunklen Nacht,
Wenn vor uns stehen,
Die immer neu unserm Herzen fehlen—
Erinnerung erwacht
An die alten Kirchen, die Hügel im Feld,
Wo sie schlafen, Vätern und Nachbarn gesellt,
In verlorener Heimat über der See—
Und an Alle, die hilflos und einsam starben,
An Alle, die sinkend im Eis verdarben,
Die keiner begrub, nur Wasser und Schnee,
Auf dem Weg unsrer Flucht,—dem Weg ohne Gnade!

Und wir ziehen im Traum verwehte Pfade
Wagen an Wagen, endloser Zug,
Der ein Volk aus der Heimat trug!

Von Norden, Von Osten kamen wir,
Über Heide und Ströme zogen wir,
Nach Westen wandernd, Greis, Frau und Kind.
Wir kamen gegangen, wir kamen gefahren,
Mit Schlitten und Bündeln, mit Hund und Karren,
Gepeitscht vom Wind, vom Schneelicht blind—
        Und Wagen an Wagen.

Zuckend wie Nordlicht am Himmel stand
Verlassener Dörfer und Städte Brand
Und um uns heulte und pfiff der Tod
Auf glühendem Ball durch die Luft getragen,
Und der Schnee wurde rot,
Und es sanken wie Garben, die hilflos starben,
Und wir zogen weiter,
                Wagen an Wagen—

Agnes Miegel

WAGON AFTER WAGON

At All Souls' Day
In the dark of night,
When they arise from the dead
Who forever are missed by our hearts—
Memory turns
To the old churches and graves in the faraway land
Where in the lost homeland across the sea
Our ancestors sleep and our friends—
And to those who died, helpless, alone,
To all those who sank beneath the ice,
Buried only by water and snow,
During our flight—the flight of the doomed!

In our dreams we wander the snow-covered roads
When in wagon after wagon, in a trek without end
A people was carried away from its land.

We came from North, from East,
Trekking across river and plain,
Trekking West—women, children, and the aged.
Walking, riding. Tired, slow,
Whipped by the storm, blinded by snow,
In dogcarts, in sleighs—while the snowstorm raged—
Wagon after wagon.

The blaze of abandoned villages and towns
Flickered like northern lights in the sky,
Death screamed and whistled as he swooped down
Upon the many who helplessly died.
And the snow turned red
Where the dead were lying like sheaves.
But we drove on,
                    wagon after wagon—

Und kamen noch einmal, trügrisches Hoffen,
Durch friedliches Land.
Tür stand uns offen
Bei jenen, die nicht unser Leiden gekannt.
Sie kamen, sie winkten, sie reichten uns Brot,
Sie luden die Not
Am warmen Herde zu sich als Gast.
Scheune und Stroh rief Müde zur Rast.
Doch wir konnten nicht bleiben.
Wir zogen vorüber,
     Wagen an Wagen.

Und hörten durch Sturm und Flockentreiben
Das Glockenlied ihrer Türme noch
Und hörten doch
Das Dröhnen des Krieges, der hinter uns zog,
Und vom Wegkreuz bog,
Blutend, mit ausgebreiteten Armen,
Sich dorngekrönter Liebe Erbarmen.
Wir konnten nicht halten, wir konnten nicht knien.
Sie kamen hinter uns, Wagen an Wagen,
Unsre Herzen nur schrien:
   O blick nach uns hin!

Wir wandern, wir wandern, endloser Zug,
Volk, das die Geißel des Krieges schlug,
Entwurzelter Wald, von der Flut getragen—
  Wohin?
    Wohin?

Hans Leip

LIED IM SCHUTT

Und als ich über die Brücke kam,
Schutt, nichts als Schutt,

Till we reached once more, Oh treacherous hope,
A peaceful zone.
Doors were flung open
By those who had not known
Our suffering.
They came and waved, they gave us bread.
But we dared not stay.
We dared not delay,
But drove on
                    wagon after wagon.

And heard while the winter storms crashed and struck
Their church bells ringing
—through tolling and singing
We heard the thunder of war, which followed us.
At the crossroad
Bleeding and with outstretched hand
Love with His crown of thorns
Bent down to us.
But we could not halt, we could not kneel,
For the march pressed on, wagon after wagon,
Only our hearts cried out:
        "Oh! Look down upon us!"

We wander, we wander, an endless trek,
People, lashed by the scourge of war,
Uprooted trees, swept to an alien shore—
        Where,
                    where shall it end?

Hans Leip

SOLDIER'S RETURN

And as I crossed the well-known bridge,
        Rubble, only rubble,

Als ich über die tote Brücke kam,
Da stand mein Vater und drohte mir,
Als wollt er sagen: Das danke ich dir!
Und suchte und suchte, was er nicht fand,
Und hob gegen mich die alte Hand,
Der ich im Wege stand.

Und als ich über die Straße kam,
Schutt, nichts als Schutt,
Als ich über die tote Straße kam,
Da stand meine Mutter und sah mich an
Und huschte und wischte hin und her,
Als wenn's in den alten Stuben wär,
Und weinte sehr.

Und als ich über den Torweg kam,
Schutt, nichts als Schutt,
Als ich über den toten Torweg kam,
Da stand mein Bruder und lachte mich aus
Und war von den Flammen ganz klein und kraus
Und sang von unsrer Kindheit ein Lied,
Von der Zeiten Glück und Unterschied
Ein trauriges Lied.

Und als ich über den Garten kam,
Schutt, nichts als Schutt,
Als ich über den toten Garten kam,
Da standen meine Schwestern drei
Und fragten, ob ich es wirklich sei
Oder nur die Vergangenheit,
Und trugen alle ein schwarzes Kleid
Wegen der toten Vergangenheit.

Und als ich über den Schulhof kam,
Schutt, nichts als Schutt,

As I crossed the dead bridge,
There stood my father with menacing face,
He seemed to say, "I owe this to you!"
He tried to find what was not there,
He shook his fists at me in despair
While I stood there.

And as I came to the well-known street,
        Rubble, only rubble,
As I came to the dead street:
There stood my mother and looked at me,
She looked—but did she really see?
She hustled and bustled and polished and swept
As in her old rooms, so spotlessly kept,
And wept.

And as I entered the entrance hall,
        Rubble, only rubble,
As I entered the dead hall:
There stood my brother with a taunting smile,
He was tiny and crisped by the fire,
And whispered and pispered a children's rhyme
About happiness and golden times,
A heartbreaking rhyme.

And as I went to our garden then,
        Rubble, only rubble,
As I went to our dead garden then:
There stood my sisters, waiting, all three,
And asked if it were really me
Or only the past.
They were in mourning, and stared aghast—
At me? At the past?

And as I came to the schoolyard,
        Rubble, only rubble,

Als ich über den toten Schulhof kam,
Da stand mein alter Lehrer so grau
Und wußte das Gute und Böse genau
Und wies mit dem Finger nach hier und dort
In der Menschheit Irrsinn und Brand und Mord
Und fand kein Wort.

Und als ich über den Kirchplatz kam,
Schutt, nichts als Schutt,
Als ich über den toten Kirchplatz kam,
Da stand am zerschmetterten Turme gebückt
Meine Liebste und hatte ein Kränzlein gepflückt
Aus verkohltem Gebälk und zerborstenem Stein
Und lächelte selig und lud mich ein,
Ihr Bräutigam zu sein.

Und als ich über das Ufer kam,
Schutt, nichts als Schutt,
Als ich über das tote Ufer kam,
Da sah ich mich selber im Wasser stehn
Und sah mich selber von dannen gehn,
So leicht, so frei, so ohne Beschwer,
Und glaubte es nicht und ging hinterher,
Als ob es im Traume wär.

Und als ich über die Ferne kam,
Schutt, nichts als Schutt,
Als ich über die tote Ferne kam,
Da sah ich die tote Stadt von fern
Und sah sie aufleuchten wie einen Stern
Und sah ihre Not und Trübsal vergehn
Und sah die Erschlagenen auferstehn
Schöner, als je ich gesehn.

Welchen Ruhm und Preis
Forderst du, unerforschliches Walten?

As I came to the dead schoolyard:
Among the ruins my teacher stood
Who always knew what was bad and good:
His hand pointed to the frenzied world,
To mankind's madness, to fury and blood,
He found no word.

And as I went to the churchyard,
  Rubble, only rubble,
As I went to the dead churchyard:
There stood my sweetheart at the gate,
Holding a wreath which she had made
From crumbled stone and blackened tree,
And smiled so sweetly and beckoned to me
To be her lover.

And as I came to the water's edge,
  Rubble, only rubble,
As I came to the water's edge:
I saw my image in the swift-running stream
And saw myself go forward—away—
So light, so free—oh, free of care!
And could not believe it, and followed there
As if in a dream.

And as I came to the distant land,
  Rubble, only rubble,
As I came to the far dead land:
I saw our city from afar,
And saw her glowing like a star,
I saw her woe and her grief were gone,
I saw her ascending, and rising she shone
Fairer than ever.

What glory, what price
Dost Thou want, Unfathomable Being?

Wie weit
Sind wir gekommen,
Was hast du uns genommen,
Ungeheuerlichkeit!
Bist du noch das ewige Licht?
So mach uns wieder jung!

O schmales grünes Reis,
Das unsere Hände halten,
Welke nicht,
Hoffnung!

Friedrich Georg Jünger

Zwischen den Säulen, sagst du, ist nichts?
Zwischen den Säulen erhebt sich
—O Herrlichkeit!—
Die zweite Ordnung von Säulen
Eine Ordnung von Säulen des Lichtes.
Wer sie nicht sieht,
Hat des Tempels Bau nicht gesehen.
Wohlgeformt von der Plinthe zum Kranz,
Mit Kelchen und Friesen
Greift der Marmor ins Licht,
Greift das Licht in die marmornen Schäfte.
Ein Zwiegespräch ist es,
Ein Gesang, hörbar, unhörbar,
Des Sichtbaren Tanz mit dem Ungesehenen.
Leere ist um mich,
Und sie schafft mit an der Fülle.

How far
Have we come?
What hast Thou NOT taken from us
Inscrutable Power?
Art Thou still The Eternal Light?
Oh, renew us!

O tender green twig
That our hands are still grasping:
Do not wilt,
Hope!

Friedrich Georg Jünger

BETWEEN THE PILLARS

Between the pillars is nothing, you say?
Between the pillars arises
—O miracle!—
Another order of columns,
An order of columns of light.
He who is not able to see them
Does not see the temple's design.
Well formed, from plinth to corona
With calix and frieze,
Marble reaches into light,
As light reaches into marble shafts.
It is a duet,
A song—audible, inaudible—
A dance of the seen with the unseen.
A void is around me
And takes part in creating abundance.

Friedrich Georg Jünger

Mit dem Saft der Maulbeere haben die Kinder
Ihre kleinen Gesichter beschmiert.
Näscher sind sie, Koster der Süßigkeit.
Sie tanzen in ihren geflickten Kleidern,
Und mit ihnen tanzt der Westwind,
Tanzt auf den Schnüren die Wäsche.
Es ist, als ob ein Hauch des wunderbaren Lebens
Die leeren Hüllen des Menschen fülle.

Gespenster, Geister, Träume.

Eine Trommel rührt sich in den mittagshellen Dörfern,
Ein Wachtelruf, der Gesang des Neuntöters
        im Schlehenbusch.
Dies alles ist einfach.
Zurückgekehrt bist du,
Zurückgekehrt an den Ausgang.
Du merkst, daß Wiege und Sarg sich ähneln.
Durchmessen der Kreis, das heißt:
Die Mitte gefunden.

Friedrich Georg Jünger

Ich steige nicht tiefer,
Als die Quelle gründet,
Das Feuer zündet,
Nicht tiefer hinab.

Von der Wurzel zur Krone
Steigen die Lieder,

Friedrich Georg Jünger

THE CIRCLE

The children smeared their little faces with mulberry juice.
They are fruit-stealers, tasters of sweetness.
They dance in their patched garments,
And the west wind dances with them
And with the washing on the line,
As if a breath of wondrous life
Fleetingly filled the empty husks of men.

Ghosts—phantoms—dreams—

A drum stirs in the noon-bright villages,
The call of a quail, the cry of a shrike in the sloebush.
All this is simple.
You have come back,
Back to the beginning,
To know that cradle and coffin look alike.
The circle is traversed: its center found.

Friedrich Georg Jünger

NO DEEPER

I descend no deeper
Than where the well springs,
The fire kindles,
No deeper than that.

From root to crown
The song rises,

Und abwärts wieder
Fällt der Gesang.

Ans Dunkle zu rühren
Und an das Lichte,
Das ist der Gedichte
Vollkommener Gang.

Friedrich Georg Jünger

DER WILDSCHWAN

Hoch über euren Kronen, ihr Eichen, zog
Der Wildschwan fort, da riß ihn ein Feuerstrahl
Herab zur Erde. Dumpf auf scholl der
Boden des Waldes von dem schweren Falle.

Wo ist, o schöne Leda, dein Buhle jetzt?
Flaum fliegt im Winde, purpurne Tropfen blühn
In Laub und Gras, die Nebel steigen
Herbstlich am Schilfe der feuchten Ufer.

Marie Luise Kaschnitz

ICH LEBTE

I

Ich lebte in einer Zeit,
Die hob sich in Wellen
Kriegauf und kriegab,
Und das Janusgesicht
Stieß mit der Panzerfaust
Ihr die bebänderten Wiegen.

And down again
The chant falls.

To touch the darkness,
To touch the light:
That is the poem's
Perfect course.

Friedrich Georg Jünger

THE WILD SWAN

High above your crowns, you oak trees, the wild swan
pursued his way till a streak of fire
snatched him down to earth. The wooded ground
resounded dully from his heavy fall.

Where is your lover now, O beautiful Leda?
Swan's-down flies in the wind, purple drops blossom
on leaves and grass; fog rises,
autumnally, in the reeds of the swampy shore.

Marie Luise Kaschnitz

I LIVED

I

I lived in a time
That rose in waves,
—up-war, down-war—
And the Janus face
Pushed the beribboned cradle
With a bazooka.

Der Tausendfüßler, das Volk,
Zog sein grünfleckiges Tarnzeug
An und aus,
Schrie, haut auf den Lukas,
Biß ins Sommergras
Und bettelte um Gnade.

. . . . .

Um den Himmel flogen
Selbständig rechnende
Geräte, zeichneten auf
Den Grad unsrer Fühllosigkeit
Den Bogen unsrer Verzweiflung.

In den Sperrstunden spielten
Abgehackte Hände Klavier
Lieblichen Mozart.

II

Und rasch war die Zeit meine Zeit,
Wer von Pferden gezogen zur Welt kam,
Verließ sie im Raumschiff.
Wem Aladins Wunderlampe
Aufs Lesebuch schien,
Entziffert im Flutlicht
Den Vers seines Alters.

Solange ich denken kann,
Gingen Uhren immer zu schnell.
Türme wuchsen sich selbst
Über den Kopf,
Läufer überholten sich selbst
Auf der Aschenbahn.

Im Echo der Zwölfuhrkanone
Erblühte das Nachmittagsrot,
Am Abend wurde der Morgen ausgeschrieen
Und im Sommer die künstliche Weihnacht.

The millipede, the people,
Donned and doffed
Their green-spotted camouflage,
Screamed, let him have it,
Bit the dust,
And groveled for grace.

. . . . .

Instruments, automatically controlled,
Circled the sky, and registered
The degree of our indifference,
The curve of our despair.

At blackout
Chopped-off hands played the piano,
Lovely Mozart.

II

And quick was the time, my time.
He who came to this world, drawn by horses,
Left in a spaceship.
Whose primer was lit up by Aladdin's lamp,
Had to decipher
The verse of his old age
In floodlight.

As far back as I can think,
Clocks always were too fast.
Towers overtowered
Themselves.
Runners outran themselves
On the cinder track.

Afternoon's rosy tints bloomed
In the echo of the siren at noon.
Evening was proclaimed at dawn,
And artificial Christmas in summer.

Schnell schoß der Same ins Kraut
Und die Knospe ins Schattenblatt,
Schnell reifte das Fruchtfleisch
Und der Wurm im Fruchtfleisch.

Mit Ruten peitschten wir
Die Jahre aus der Welt
Und traten voll Ungeduld
Unter die Erde die Toten.

Es wurde gebaut übernacht
Ein tausendfenstriges Haus
Am Hudson am Main
An den Ufern des Bosporus
Und ein Ding, es zu wandeln in Staub
Übernacht.

. . . . .

V

Und doch in meiner Zeit
Kamen Kinder aus Mütterleibern,
Schleimige Lurche noch immer,
Und wurden, auch die späteren Ungeheuer,
Mit Weihwasser begrüßt
Und Schrei der Freude.

Mund auf Mund gepreßt
Der Liebenden bäumte sich auf
Gegen die Einsamkeit,
Und ein altes Entzücken
Überströmte noch immer
Glitzernd das Steinfeld.

Angst zu sterben
Und Angst zu leben
Hielten sich die Waage noch immer.

Quickly the seed ran into leaves
And buds into shadow-foliage.
Quickly the fruit ripened
And the maggot in it.

We whipped the years
Out of the world
And full of impatience
We trampled the dead into the ground.

Everywhere they built houses
With a thousand windows,
On the Hudson, on the Main,
On the edge of the Bosporus,
And also a thing to turn them into dust,
Overnight.

. . . . .

V

And yet in this my time
Children slipped from their mothers' wombs
Slippery newts as of old
And were greeted with holy water
And cries of joy,
Even the future monsters.

Lovers, mouth pressed to mouth,
Rose against loneliness
And ancient delight
Still flooded, glittering,
The stony field.

Fear of dying
And fear of living
Still counterpoised each other.

Natur trug unbekümmert ihr altes Gewand
Herzzerreißende Schönheit.
Das Leben war noch immer ein Geheimnis.
Der Tod ein andres.

Marie Luise Kaschnitz

LIEBE SONNE

Wir glauben an diese
Unsere große
Freiheit zu sterben
Häuser unsere
Einstürzen zu lassen
Weingärten unsere
Brach—

Wir glauben es zwänge
Uns niemand aufzuerstehen
Späterhin in das Licht
In die gewaltige
Anstrengung ewigen Lebens.

Wir glauben es stünde bei uns
Niemanden mehr zu lieben
Und hintreiben zu lassen endlich
Erkaltet in kalten Schwärmen
Diesen unseren Stern.

Aber die unverminderte
Tägliche Zeugenschaft
Küssender Lippen
Liebe Sonne
Schöne Erde
Ewig ewig
Weiß es besser.

Nature, unconcerned, wore her
Age-old garment of heart-rending beauty.
Life still was a secret,
Death another one.

Marie Luise Kaschnitz

DEAR SUN

We believe in this
Our great
Freedom to die
Houses our houses
Let fall in ruin
Vineyards our vineyards
Left to lie fallow—

We believe that nobody
Can force us later
To rise into the light
To the tremendous
Effort of eternal life.

We believe it is in our power
Not to love anymore
And to let drift at last—
Cold amid cold clusters of stars
This our own star.

But the unabated
Daily evidence
Of kissing lips
Of dear sun
Fair earth
Forever and ever
Knows better.

Marie Luise Kaschnitz

Als sie den Dichter begraben haben
War einer da, der für ein Wochenblatt
Einige Aufnahmen machte. Man sah sie später.
Den steilen Sarg, wie um ein mächtiges Haupt
Gezimmert, und den aufgeworfenen Wall,
Die Schaufel Erde in der Hand des Freundes,
Verwackelt, weil die Hand gezittert hatte.
Es war, alles in allem, eine klägliche Feier.
Abwesend war das Oberhaupt der Stadt
Abwesend waren die Herren der Akademie.
Die Blumen waren aus Stroh und die Kränze stachlig.
Wer stürbe gerne in der Rosenzeit?
Der Pfarrer sprach sehr lang. Die Kinder übten
Verstohlen still, auf einem Bein zu stehen.
Einige waren gekommen, die niemand erblickte.
Sieben Dryaden, zwei Nymphen, ein Feuersalamander.
Nicht, daß der Dichter sie besungen hätte
Doch sie schienen zu glauben, sie gehörten dazu.
Die Gäste hatten Angst sich zu erkälten
ein Toter zieht den Anderen ins Grab . . .
Sie schlossen ihre Mäntel, starrten gedankenlos
Die Wolke an, die über ihre Köpfe
Dahinfuhr, schwarz und herrlich—
Die schöne Wolke, dachte der Photograph
Und machte eine Aufnahme privat.
Eine fünfzigstel Sekunde, Blende zehn.
Doch auf der Platte war dann nichts zu sehen.

Marie Luise Kaschnitz

BURIAL OF A POET

When they buried the poet,
A man was there who took some pictures
For a weekly. We saw them later on.
The high coffin as if framed around a mighty head,
The cast-up wall,
The shovel with earth in the hand of a friend
—blurred—since the hand had trembled.
It was a piteous ceremony, all in all.
The burgomaster was absent.
The gentlemen of the Academy were absent.
The flowers were of straw, and the wreaths were prickly.
Who likes to die in the time of roses?
The minister spoke too long. The children,
Furtively quiet, practiced balancing on one leg.
Some others had come and nobody laid eyes on them:
Seven dryads, two nymphs, a salamander.
Not that the poet sang of them
But they seemed to believe they belonged there.
The mourners were afraid they might catch cold—
"A dead man will draw another man into the grave. . ."
They buttoned their coats, unthinkingly gazing
At the cloud that sailed above their heads,
Dark and magnificent—
Such a beautiful cloud, thought the photographer
And privately he took a picture—
One fiftieth of a second, lens opening, ten.
But, it turned out, the cloud eluded him.

Peter Huchel

IN DER HEIMAT

Zeit mit rostiger Sense,
Spät erst zogest du fort,
Den Hohlweg hinauf, den ich einst ging,
Grau in der Schar der Fliehenden.
Über uns der Himmel wie dünnes Wasser.
Ein weißer Stein ertrank.
War es der Mond? Oder das Auge der Ödnis?

Am Gräbergebüsch klagte die Dämmerung.
Sie hüllte ihr Tuch,
Aus Gras und Nebel grob gewebt,
Um Helme und Knochen.
Die erste Frühe, umkrustet von Eis,
Warf blinkende Scherben ins Schilf.
Schweigend schob der Fischer
Den Kahn in den Fluß und holte uns über.
Es klagte die frierende Stimme des Wassers,
Das so viel Tote flößte hinunter.

Wer aber begrub sie, im frostigen Lehm,
In Asche und Schlamm,
Die alte Fußspur der Not?
Im Kahlschlag des Krieges glänzt Ackererde.
Überall stand das Lebendige auf,
Wo der Mensch die steinige Öde bezwang,
Schützend mit windauskämmender Hecke
Den Halm, die lockere Krume.
Und Weizen sucht mit saugender Wurzel
Die schwere Erde, die alles gebäret;
Es drängt die quellende Kraft der Saat
Und herrscht, wo stauende Nässe war.

Peter Huchel

HOMELAND

Time with rusty scythe,
Only late you drew away
The sunken road, uphill, where I once walked
Gray in the band of fugitives.
The sky above us like diluted water.
A white stone was drowning.
Was that the moon? Or the eye of the wasteland?

At the bushy graves Dusk was lamenting.
She wrapped her shawl,
Coarsely woven from grass and fog,
Around helmets and bones.
Early dawn, crusty with ice,
Threw glittering splinters into the reeds.
Silently the fisherman pushed
His boat into the river and carried us over.
The shivering voice of the river lamented,
So many dead were floating down river.

But who then buried, in frosty loam,
In ashes and mud,
The old footprint of grief?
In the clearing of war, arable land is gleaming.
Everywhere life is rising
Where man conquered the stony wasteland,
Protecting blades, the loose topsoil,
With wind-combing hedges.
Wheat with sucking roots is seeking
The heavy soil that brings forth everything.
The swelling force of seed is pressing,
Reigning now where dampness stagnated.

II

Weißwollige Distel kündet den Sommer.
Die Frauen raufen den Flachs.
Und an der gesprengten Brücke vorbei
Treibt hügelhinauf
Der Hund die Schafe ins weite Gehüt.

Schön ist die Heimat,
Wenn über der grünen Messingscheibe
Des Teiches der Kranich schreit
Und das Gold sich häuft
Im blauen Oktobergewölbe;
Wenn Korn und Milch in der Kammer schlafen,
Die rußige Schmiede des Alls
Beginnt ihr Feuer zu schüren.
Vom Amboß der Nacht
Und fallend auf den Schatten der Fledermäuse
Sprühen die Funken.
War es nicht immer die Nacht,
Die in Donnern hallende Nacht,
Die das glühende Eisen
Der Morgenröte schuf?

Noch stehen am Hohlweg
Die beiden Pappeln
Und ragen ins Licht
Wie Fühler der Erde.
Sie spüren das Wehen des Schilfs
Und den harten Atem des Manns,
der unten am Hang den Schälpflug wendet,
Die Stoppel stürzt.
Er pflügt auch mein Herz
Und senkt sein Saatgut in mein Wort.

II

The white-woolly thistle announces summer.
Women are combing flax.
A dog drives sheep
Past the demolished bridge
Uphill to the wide pasture.

My homeland is beautiful
When cranes are calling across
The green brazen disk of the pond,
And gold is being heaped
In the blue dome of October,
When grain and milk are sleeping in the chamber,
When the rusty forge of the world
Is beginning to stir the fire.
Sparks are flying
From the anvil of night,
Falling upon the shadows of bats.
Was it not always the night,
The night resounding with thunder,
That created the glowing iron
Of dawn?

The two poplars are still standing
At the sunken road,
Towering in the light
Like feelers of the earth.
They feel the waving of the reeds
And the hard breath of the man
Who is turning his paring plow
There at the slope.
The stubble is being turned over.
He is plowing my heart too,
Sinking his seed into my word.

Peter Huchel

WINTERPSALM

für Hans Mayer

Da ich ging bei träger Kälte des Himmels
Und ging hinab die Straße zum Fluß,
Sah ich die Mulde im Schnee,
Wo nachts der Wind
Mit flacher Schulter gelegen.
Seine gebrechliche Stimme,
In den erstarrten Ästen oben,
Stieß sich am Trugbild weißer Luft:
„Alles Verscharrte blickt mich an.
Soll ich es heben aus dem Staub
Und zeigen dem Richter? Ich schweige.
Ich will nicht Zeuge sein."
Sein Flüstern erlosch,
Von keiner Flamme genährt.

Wohin du stürzt, o Seele,
Nicht weiß es die Nacht. Denn da ist nichts
Als vieler Wesen stumme Angst.
Der Zeuge tritt hervor. Es ist das Licht.

Ich stand auf der Brücke,
Allein vor der trägen Kälte des Himmels.
Atmet noch schwach,
Durch die Kehle des Schilfrohrs
Der vereiste Fluß?

Peter Huchel

WINTER PSALM

for Hans Mayer

As I walked in the listless chill of the sky,
And walked down the street to the river,
I saw the hollow in the snow
Where the wind with his shallow shoulder
Had been lying last night.
His frail voice in the brittle boughs
Was knocking against white phantoms of air:
"All that is buried, is looking at me.
Shall I lift it up from the dust
And show it to the judge? I am silent.
I won't be a witness."
His whispering died away,
No flame sustained it.

Whereto do you plunge, O soul?
The night does not know for there is nothing
But the silent fear of many beings.
The witness steps forward: it is the light.

I stood on the bridge,
Alone under the listless chill of the sky.
Is the frost-bound river
Still breathing, weakly,
Through its windpipes of reed?

Günter Eich

NACHHUT

Steh auf, steh auf!
Wir werden nicht angenommen,
die Botschaft kam mit dem Schatten der Sterne.

Es ist Zeit zu gehen wie die andern.
Sie stellten ihre Straßen und leeren Häuser
unter den Schutz des Mondes. Er hat wenig Macht.

Unsere Worte werden von der Stille aufgezeichnet.
Die Kanaldeckel heben sich um einen Spalt.
Die Wegweiser haben sich gedreht.

Wenn wir uns erinnerten an die Wegmarken der Liebe,
Ablesbar auf Wasserspiegeln und im Wehen des Schnees!
Komm, ehe wir blind sind!

Günter Eich

AUGENBLICK IM JUNI

Wenn das Fenster geöffnet ist,
Vergänglichkeit mit dem Winde hereinweht,
mit letzten Blütenblättern der roten Kastanie
und dem Walzer „Faszination"
von neunzehnhundertundvier,
wenn das Fenster geöffnet ist
und den Blick freigibt auf Floßhafen und Stapelholz,
das immer bewegte Blattgewirk der Akazie—
wie ein Todesurteil ist der Gedanke an dich.
Wer wird Deine Brust küssen
und deine geflüsterten Worte kennen?

Günter Eich

REAR GUARD

Get up! Get up!
We shall not be accepted,
the message came with the shadows of the stars.

It is time to leave as the others did.
They committed their streets and empty houses
to the care of the moon. She has little power.

Our words are recorded by the stillness.
The lids of the sewers are being raised a crack.
The signposts have turned around.

If we only could remember the landmarks of love,
readable on the reflecting water or the drift of snow!
Let us go before we become blind.

Günter Eich

MOMENT IN JUNE

When the window is open
and impermanence drifts into the room with the wind,
with the last petals of the red chestnut tree
and the waltz "Fascination"
from nineteen hundred and four,
when the window is open
and the view is free over the rafts, the floating timber,
and the forever-swaying tapestry of acacia leaves—
the thought of you is like a death warrant.
Who will kiss your breast
and know your whispered words?

Wenn das Fenster geöffnet ist
und das Grauen der Erde hereinweht—
Das Kind mit zwei Köpfen,
—während der eine schläft, schreit der andere—
es schreit über die Welt hin
und erfüllt die Ohren meiner Liebe mit Entsetzen.
(Man sagt, die Mißgeburten nähmen seit Hiroshima zu.)

Wenn das Fenster geöffnet ist, gedenke ich derer,
die sich liebten im Jahre neunzehnhundertundvier
und der Menschen des Jahres dreitausend,
zahnlos, haarlos.

Wem gibst du den zerrinnenden Blick, der einst mein war?
Unser Leben, es fähret schnell dahin als flögen wir davon,
und in den Abgründen wohnt verborgen das Glück.

Günter Eich

ENDE AUGUST

Mit weißen Bäuchen hängen die toten Fische
zwischen Entengrütze und Schilf.
Die Krähen haben Flügel, dem Tod zu entrinnen.
Manchmal weiß ich, daß Gott
am meisten sich sorgt um das Dasein der Schnecke.
Er baut ihr ein Haus. Uns aber liebt er nicht.

Eine weiße Staubfahne zieht am Abend der Omnibus,
wenn er die Fußballmannschaft heimfährt.
Der Mond glänzt im Weidengestrüpp,
vereint mit dem Abendstern.
Wie nahe bist du, Unsterblichkeit, im Fledermausflügel,
im Scheinwerfer-Augenpaar,
das den Hügel herab sich naht.

When the window is open
and the world's horror drifts into the room—
the two-headed child
—while one head is asleep, the other one is screaming—
screaming across the world,
filling my loved one's ears with terror.
(They say deformities are increasing since Hiroshima.)

When the window is open I think of those
who loved in the year nineteen hundred and four
and of man in the year three thousand,
toothless, hairless.

To whom do you direct your languishing gaze which once
sought only me?
Our life is soon cut off, and we fly away,
and happiness lives hidden in the abyss.

Günter Eich

END OF AUGUST

White-bellied dead fish are hanging
among duckweed and reeds.
Crows have wings to escape death.
Sometimes I know that God
is most concerned about the existence of snails.
He built houses for them. But he does not love us.

At evening, the bus drags a flag of white dust
as it carries home the football team.
In the willow thicket the moon glows,
linked to the evening star.
How near you are, eternity, in a bat's wing,
in the headlight-pair of eyes
drawing nearer down the hill.

Günter Eich

JAPANISCHER HOLZSCHNITT

Ein rosa Pferd,
gezäumt und gesattelt—
für wen?

Wie nah der Reiter auch sei,
er bleibt verborgen.

Komm du für ihn,
tritt in das Bild ein
und ergreif die Zügel!

Günter Eich

DIE HERKUNFT DER WAHRHEIT

Die Herkunft der Wahrheit bedenken:
ihre mit Sand behafteten Wurzeln,
ihre Fußspur,
die meßbare Bewegung der Luft,
wenn sie als Vogel kam.

Einsichten aus Pervitin,
zum Abflug gesammelt mit den Schwalben.
Fort, fort, in den Abend und übers Gebirge!

Andere, Steinmetzzeichen im Laub,
nur begreiflich dem Schlafe.
Und eins mit den Scherzen der Großmütter:
mach die Augen zu,
was du dann siehst
gehört dir.

Günter Eich

JAPANESE WOODCUT

A pink horse,
bridled and saddled—
for whom?

However near the rider may be,
he remains hidden.

You come in his place,
enter the picture
and seize the reins.

Günter Eich

THE PROVENANCE OF TRUTH

To ponder the provenance of truth:
its sand-encumbered roots,
its footprints,
the measurable motion of air
when it comes as a bird.

Visions, gained from benzedrine,
gathered for flight with the swallows.
Away, away, into the evening and over the mountains!

Others, stonecutter's marks under the leaves,
understandable only in sleep.
And, at one with the little jokes of grandmothers:
Close your eyes,
what you can see then—
that is yours.

Rudolf Hagelstange

DER GLETSCHER

Plötzlich, inmitten der Nacht,
die um die funkelnde Achse des Mondes
pfau-blau ihr Rad schlägt, begreifst du:
Zeit ist vieles und nichts. Auch der Ort ist
groß und gering, denn beide
höhlt und benagt sie
das einzig Beständige:
Die große Bewegung.

Leise
in weltferner Stille
atmet der Gletscher,
flutet unendlich die eisige Lunge,
überflutet den Ort und die Zeit,
stillt und bedenkt und durchblutet
die wartenden Täler.

Wer hat die mächtigen Flanken gebildet,
an denen, abwärtstastend,
das Licht seinen Tag mißt? —Antwort
hallt aus dem tosenden Fall,
flüstern Myriaden schmelzender Tropfen,
eingesprengt ins Atom einer Sekunde:

Alles ist Fließen. Lebendiges
reißt das Tote mit sich, und Totes
trägt
auf dem Kadaver, dem treibenden,
strahlendes Leben.

Rudolf Hagelstange

THE GLACIER

Suddenly, in the depth of the night
which strikes a wheel of peacock-blue
around the brilliant axis of the moon, you grasp this:
time is everything, and is nothing. And place too is
great and yet insignificant, for both
are denuded and hollowed
by the only permanence:
the great motion.

Softly,
in secluded silence,
the glacier breathes;
the icy lung flows unendingly,
overflows time and place,
calms, and remembers, and suffuses
the waiting valleys.

Who formed the powerful flanks
by which, groping downward,
light measures its day? —the thundering fall
echoes the answer,
millions of melting drops whisper it,
interspersed into the atom of a second:

Change is the only permanence. Life
seizes on the decayed, and death
carries
upon its drifting carcass
radiant life.

Rudolf Hagelstange

DAS WORT

Nimm dieses Ding, dies Wort da! Wirf es hin,
dort auf den Stein, und prüf, ob es zerspringt.
Wirfs wie ein Messer
an den Baum—noch besser:
wirfs auf die Brust des Nächsten, ob es steckt!
Und ob es tief, tief in sein Leben dringt.
Es muß so fest im roten Muskel haften,
daß, zöge ers hinaus, die Ränder klafften
und sich nicht wieder schlössen.
Doch gib acht! Der Griff ist alt,
die Klinge stumpf vom vielen Schneiden,
vom Schnitzen, Schälen, Schaben. Nur die Spitze
hält alte Kraft.—Oder auch nicht.
Vielleicht ist nur das eine noch: Gewicht,
Gewicht von Eisen, und von deiner Hand
der feste Wurf und deines Auges
gezielter Blick. Gleichviel:
Du mußt es werfen, wie es ist.
Verwirf es, fällt es nieder in den Sand.
Und steckt es tief—so taug es!

Hilde Domin

NUR EINE ROSE ALS STÜTZE

Ich richte mir ein Zimmer ein in der Luft
unter den Akrobaten und Vögeln:
mein Bett auf dem Trapez des Gefühls
wie ein Nest im Wind
auf der äußersten Spitze des Zweigs.

Rudolf Hagelstange

THE WORD

Take this thing, this word! Throw it down,
there upon the stone, and see if it will break.
Throw it like a knife
at a tree—even better:
throw it at your neighbor's heart, see if it will hold
and will penetrate deep, deep into his life!
It must stay so tightly in the red muscle
that the edges will remain severed
and not close again
if he pulls it out.
But be careful! The handle is old,
the edge blunt from much cutting,
from whittling, paring, scraping. Only the point
holds the old force. —Or maybe not.
Perhaps there is only one thing left: weight,
weight of iron, and the strong thrust
of your hand, and the well-aimed glance
of your eyes. No matter:
you must throw it as it is.
Cast it away if it falls down into the sand.
But if it cuts deeply—then it may serve.

Hilde Domin

ONLY A ROSE FOR SUPPORT

I set up a room for myself in the air
among acrobats and birds:
I make my bed upon the trapeze of emotion,
like a nest in the wind
at the outer end of a bough.

Ich kaufe mir eine Decke aus der zartesten Wolle
der sanftgescheitelten Schafe die
im Mondlicht
wie schimmernde Wolken
über die feste Erde ziehn.

Ich schließe die Augen und hülle mich ein
in das Vlies der verläßlichen Tiere.
Ich will den Sand unter den kleinen Hufen spüren
und das Klicken des Riegels hören,
der die Stalltür am Abend schließt.

Aber ich liege in Vogelfedern, hoch ins Leere gewiegt.
Mir schwindelt. Ich schlafe nicht ein.
Meine Hand
greift nach einem Halt und findet
nur eine Rose als Stütze.

Hilde Domin

AUF WOLKENBÜRGSCHAFT

Ich habe Heimweh nach einem Land
in dem ich niemals war,
wo alle Bäume und Blumen
mich kennen,
in das ich niemals geh,
doch wo sich die Wolken
meiner
genau erinnern,
ein Fremder, der sich
in keinem Zuhause
ausweinen kann.

I buy a blanket of the daintiest wool
of soft-combed sheep which,
in moonlight,
move across the firm earth
like shimmering clouds.

I close my eyes and wrap myself
into the fleece of reliable animals,
I want to feel the sand under their little hoofs
and hear the click of the bolt
as it locks the barn door at night.

But I am lying in bird feathers, cradled high in emptiness,
I grow dizzy. I cannot sleep.
My hand
reaches out and finds
only a rose for support.

Hilde Domin

ON A CLOUD'S AFFIDAVIT

I am homesick for a country,
    —I have never been there—
where the trees and flowers
know me
    —I shall never go there—
but where the clouds
remember me
distinctly,
a stranger who
has no home
where he can cry.

Ich fahre
nach Inseln ohne Hafen,
ich werfe die Schlüssel ins Meer
gleich nach der Ausfahrt.
Ich komme nirgends an.
Mein Segel ist wie ein Spinnweb im Wind,
aber es reißt nicht.
Und jenseits des Horizonts,
wo die großen Vögel
am Ende ihres Flugs
die Schwingen in der Sonne trocknen,
liegt ein Erdteil
wo sie mich aufnehmen müssen,
ohne Paß,
auf Wolkenbürgschaft.

Hilde Domin

MORGENS UND ABENDS II

Die Wiesen, die Augen
früh und spät
so naß.

Dazwischen
ist Tag.

Peter Jokostra

MITSAMT SEINEN ENGELN

Mitsamt seinen Engeln
starb er lächelnd im Frühlicht,

I sail
to islands without harbors,
I throw my keys into the sea
right after leaving.
I arrive nowhere.
My sail is like a spider's web in the wind
but it does not tear.
And, beyond the horizon,
where the great birds,
at the end of their flight,
dry their wings in the sun,
there lies a continent
where they must accept me
without a passport—
on a cloud's affidavit.

Hilde Domin

MORNING AND EVENING II

Meadows, eyes,
so wet
early and late.

In between
is the day.

Peter Jokostra

TOGETHER WITH HIS ANGELS

Together with his angels
he died, smiling, at dawn;

die Nacht der Sierra
wie ein Kranz schwarzer Tulpen
im Rücken.

O, gehe nicht hin!
Sie töten jetzt Lorca
mitsamt seinen Engeln.

Stierengel, rot,
auf Andalusiens Gärten gestürzt,
mit der zuckenden Flamme des Schnees
im angstweißen Haar.

Beim Schlaf meiner Schwester:
sieh, wie er lächelt!

Das taten die Knechte
dem Fürsten der Berge
in blindem Gehorsam.
Sie taten es blind.

Peter Jokostra

DIE ZEIT IST DEIN JÄGER

Stirn
gegen das Fenster des Windes gelehnt,
geschmückt
mit den Zähnen des Wolfs:
flieh aus der Feindschaft des Worts,
das dich sucht und dich trifft.

Es schlägt dich
mit feurigem Kuß auf den Mund.
Es filtert

against his back
the night of the Sierra
like a wreath of black tulips.

Oh, do not go there!
Now they are killing Lorca
together with his angels.

Bull-angels, red,
tearing at Andalusia's gardens,
a twitching flame of snow
in fear-white hair.

By the soul of my sister:
see, how he smiles!

Serfs, in blind obedience,
did that
to the prince of the mountains.
They did it blindly.

Peter Jokostra

TIME IS YOUR HUNTER

Forehead
leaning against the window of the wind,
decorated
with wolf's teeth:
flee from the enmity of words
that search you out and crush you.

They strike
your mouth with a fiery kiss,
filtering poison

sein Gift in die Wunden,
die frisch sind und tief
vom Wolfsbiß im Wald der Gefühle,
der sich hinter dir schließt.

Du Stirn,
beringt von den Schatten der Nacht:
es gibt keinen Morgen für dich,
denn die Zeit ist dein Jäger.

Sie findet dich immer.
Sie freut sich der Falle.
Der Wind schlägt sie zu.

Peter Jokostra

LAST DER EWIGKEIT

Messer Fluß.
Schöne Schneide Fluß.
Blitzend, aasig, voll Schwärze.
Mein großer Scharlatan,
wimpernlos gleitender Traum,
verfolgt von Schatten,
verrinnend im Licht.

Wer siedet
die zärtliche Blume des Winds,
wenn der Meiler unsrer Erinnerung
ausgeblasen ist von dem stärkeren
Feuer des Todes?

Sonne am Steilhang
duftet herb nach Regen und Lack.

into wounds
that are fresh and deep
from the bite of the wolf in the forest of emotion
that closes behind you.

Forehead,
ringed with night's shadows:
there is no morning for you,
time is your hunter.

Time always finds you
and enjoys the trap.
The wind slams it shut.

Peter Jokostra

BURDEN OF ETERNITY

River, a knife.
Lovely keen-edged river.
Flickering, foul, filled with darkness.
My great charlatan,
gliding dream without eyelashes,
pursued by shadows,
seeping away in light.

Who is scalding
the tender bloom of the wind
when the kiln of remembrance
is quenched by the stronger
fire of death?

Sun at the slope
harshly fragrant of resin and rain.

Mond schmilzt jedes Lächeln ein,
wenn es zur Maske verwandelt
groß über uns nachts
nach Vergänglichkeit schreit.

Hans Egon Holthusen

aus ACHT VARIATIONEN ÜBER ZEIT UND TOD

II

Liebe liebt sich den Tod. Wie muß die Seele erschrecken,
Wenn sie sich stößt an dem unsicher schlagenden Muskel
    des Herzens,
Wenn sie an sich heruntersieht und diese Hände
    gewahr wird,
Füße und Hüften und die plumpe Deutlichkeit
    des Geschlechts!
Dies ist ein Leib, der schlafen will, sterblich, marode,
    von Gestern und Morgen
Geschleift und gepreßt in ein Wann und Wo. Verwühlt
    in die Kissen,
Bangend und fragend: Was soll aus mir werden? Was soll
    aus der Mutter
Werden, was aus dem Bruder? (Er kann sich selbst nicht
    ertragen.)
Alles ist wie im Fallen, kopfüber und schief. Und die Seele
    Hungert nach Sicherheit.

IV

Heute noch haben wir Welt vor Augen. Wir haben
Herbst, ein Gären im Blut von verlorner und kommender
Zeit und gelbe Kastanienblätter im Hof.
Alle stimmen darin überein, daß es schön ist,
    hinauszugehen.
Kinder, vier Jahre alt, kosten für eine Sekunde,

Moon melts down every smile
when it is turned into a mask, huge,
screaming at night above us
for impermanence.

Hans Egon Holthusen

from VARIATIONS ON TIME AND DEATH

II

Love courts death. How the soul must be frightened
When it collides with the unsteadily beating muscle,
        the heart,
When it looks down and perceives these hands,
Feet and hips, and the blunt plainness of sex!
A body, needing sleep, mortal, exhausted, dragged
        and pressed
By yesterday and by tomorrow into a When and a Where.
        Fidgeting in the pillows,
Apprehensive and questioning: what will happen to me?
        What to the mother? The brother?
(He cannot suffer himself.)
Everything seems to be falling, head foremost, awry.
And the soul hungers for safety.

IV

Today, though, we have this world before our eyes.
We have autumn,
Our blood in a ferment with lost and coming time,
Yellow chestnut leaves in the yard.
People agree how pleasant it is to go out.
Children, four years old, taste for a second

Was sie ein Leben lang suchen werden und niemals besitzen:
Herbst und Heimat, die Heimat im Staube, das Wohnen
Dicht an der Rinde der Erde, die vorgeburtliche Landschaft,
Bergland, Marsch oder Geest und schwärzlich gesprenkelten
    Sand.
Kopfsteinpflaster, Wacholder und Birken, eine einsame
    Straße
Quer durch die Heide, eine Magd in schwarzen, wollenen
    Socken,
Die Schürze voll Ziegengeruch .... Man nennt es im Alter
    die Kindheit.
Spät ist, nach durchregneter Nacht, die Klarheit
    des Morgens,
Süßer Moder, geklärt in der Luft, Oktober, Ariadne und
    Theseus,
Golden, ein Rondo von Mozart, eine goldene Figurine
    in Moll.
Dies ist die Zeit, in der eine Freundin aus einer anderen
Stadt, eine Freundin, deren letzten Brief du nicht
    beantwortet hast,
Sich von einer steinernen Brüstung hinab auf die Straße
    stürzt.
Niemand wird es erfahren, wie der Himmel sich damals
    verfärbte,
Wie alle Fenster sich glasig und frostig verschlossen,
Niemand wird wissen, wie an diesem Sonntag es möglich
    war,
Daß aus dem goldenen Rondo der Tod erklang.

Karl Krolow

aus GEDICHTE GEGEN DEN TOD

VI

In einem Antlitz das Flackern der Freude,
Stilles Schiff, das ausfährt, um nicht heimzukehren:

What they shall seek all their lives, yet never shall own:
Harvest time and home, home in the dust,
Close to the earth's crust, prenatal landscape,
Highlands, marshy and dry land, or black-dappled sand,
Cobblestones, juniper and birches, a lonely road
Straight across the moor, a servant in black woolen
        stockings,
Her apron smelling of goats . . . . In old age one calls it
        childhood.
The clearness of morning came late, after it rained all night,
Sweet moldy fragrance, cleansed in the air, October,
        Ariadne and Theseus,
Golden, a rondo from Mozart, a golden figurine in a
        minor key.
This is the time when a friend in another city,
A friend whose last letter you did not answer,
Throws herself down to the pavement from the
        stone balcony.
Nobody will ever learn how the sky then turned pale,
How all the windows wrapped themselves up,
        glassy and frosty,
Nobody will know how it was possible on that Sunday
That from the golden rondo death rang out.

Karl Krolow

from POEMS AGAINST DEATH

VI

The flicker of joy in a face,
A quiet ship that puts to sea not to return:

So kommt der Abend.

Sein Leben wiegt nicht schwer auf der Schulter.
Goldgewölke im Arm, ist er da;
Und der Tod hat noch einmal Geduld:
Ein Geisterseher, dem die eigene Haut feindlich ist,
Solange die Wasseraloe mit weißem Schoß blüht
Und die Dämmerung leicht wie eine Sandwespe ist.

Das Dunkel bewegt seine Lippen.
Es ist schön, wie die Frau, die es nicht gibt.
Unsicher macht es den Tod, den sein Flüstern eine Zeitlang
    abwendet.

So kommt der Abend.
Sein Leben wiegt leicht auf der Schulter.

Und die Nacht hat die Farbe von Jennys Brauen.
Sie gleicht nicht der Freundin, die ihre Parfüms wechselt.
Sie gleicht nicht der Freundin, in deren Augen Elmsfeuer
    huschen.
Sie hat kleine Zähne, die glänzen.
Sie hat einen Mund aus Jubel und Stille.

Und der Tod hat noch einmal Geduld ...

Karl Krolow

HAND VORM GESICHT...

Hand vorm Gesicht! Sie hält
Kurz nur das Sterben ab.
Grube im Nacken fällt,
Beere am Aronstab.

Thus comes evening.

His life does not weigh heavily upon our shoulders.
He is there, gold clouds in his arms;
And death is patient once more:
A seer whose own body is at enmity with him,
As long as the water aloe is abloom with white thalamus
And dusk is weightless like a sand wasp.

Darkness moves its lips,
Beautiful as a woman who never existed.
Death wavers, turned away for a while by the whispering.

Thus comes evening.
His life weighs but lightly upon our shoulders.

And night has the color of Jenny's eyebrows.
She is not like the friend who changes her perfume,
She is not like the friend whose eyes are flashing with
        St. Elmo's fire.
She has small teeth that glisten.
She has a mouth of joy and calm.

And death is patient once more . . . .

Karl Krolow

HAND BEFORE THE FACE

Hand before face!
But death will not stop.
The nape of my neck is numb,
Arum berries drop.

Rose am leichten Stock
Wird unterm Finger Staub.
Leuchtendes Kirschgeflock
Ist schon des Windes Raub.

Ratloser Mund! Er schweigt,
Ins Schwinden still gedehnt,
Wenn sich mein Schatten zeigt,
Süß an die Luft gelehnt.

Wenn träg die Pappel samt,
Löwenzahnlampe lischt,
Vieles bleibt unbenannt,
Wie sichs in Trauer mischt.

Wie es sich ungenau
Hin zum Vergehen drängt,
Faltermann, Falterfrau,
Mutlos im Lichte schwenkt.

Über mir weiß ich schon
Stimmen aus schwarzem Schall,
Laubhaft gehauchten Ton,
Und spür den Stirnverfall.

Rückwärts mit leisem Schrei
Stürz ich ins Leere hin,
Hart hinterm Tod vorbei.
Fühl daß ichs nicht mehr bin.

Karl Krolow

GEWITTERLANDSCHAFT

Der rote Schatten des Milans
Zerfällt unter Schirmakazien.

Rose of the brier bough
Turns dust in my hand—
Glistening cherry-foam
Is prey of the wind.

Perplexed mouth! Silent,
Seems hardly to be there,
My shadow is leaning
Sweetly against air.

The seeds of dandelion
Drift in the wind—
Much is left undefined,
Confused in lament.

How they throng vaguely
Into decay and night,
A pair of butterflies
Swerve timid in the light.

I feel above me now
Voices of umber-gray,
Leaflike hushed sound—
I feel myself decay.

Backward with a low scream
I plunge into emptiness
And know myself no more.
—I almost touched death.

Karl Krolow

SULTRY LANDSCAPE

The red shadow of the falcon
Dissolves under the acacias.

Man kann das Eidechsen-Gestein
Nicht anfassen,
Ohne sich zu verbrennen.
Große Käfer umzingeln
Das Licht der heißen Gebüsche.
Eine blaue Flamme
Wandert am Straßenrand.
Wer jetzt ruft,
Bekommt nie wieder Antwort.
Die fensterlosen Häuser
wenden sich ab.
In schwarzen Nischen
Hocken Katzen.
Schon knistert ihr Fell
Im ersten Blitz.

Karl Krolow

DIE FREIHEIT

Sie flieht vorüber, in sich gekehrt.

Die Leute sagen, sie habe den bösen Blick.
Aber sie hörte in der Nacht
Das Gespräch mechanischer Waffen.
Sie sah gerade eben noch in der schneidenden Luft
Die Zeit als großen Vogel,
Der davonfliegt: die Hoffnung.
Sie sah das alte Blut aus dem Boden steigen
Und sich mit neuem verbinden.

Sie flieht vorüber, in sich gekehrt.

Die Leute sagen, sie habe den bösen Blick.
Aber plötzlich waren aus den Hüften

One cannot touch
The lizard-rocks
Without burning one's fingers.
Large beetles encircle
The light of hot bushes.
A blue flame
Wanders to the edge of the road.
He who calls out now
Shall never be answered.
The windowless houses
Turn away.
In black recesses
Cats are crouching,
Their fur already crackling
With the first lightning.

Karl Krolow

GODDESS FREEDOM

She flees past, lost in herself.

People say: she has the evil eye.
In the night she heard
Machine guns talking.
She spied already in the cutting air
Time, like a large bird,
Flying away .... Hope.
She saw old blood rising from the ground
Mingling with new blood.

She flees past, lost in herself.

People say: she has the evil eye.
But suddenly machine guns

Maschinenpistolen gewachsen.
Noch die Statuen hatten
Auf sie gefeuert.
In jedermanns Arme
War der Tod gelegt.

Sie flieht vorüber, in sich gekehrt.

An der Ecke wartet auf sie
Der schwarze Wegelagerer:
Gewalt, mit unbiegsamem Metall
In den Fäusten!

Karl Krolow

ROBINSON

Immer wieder strecke ich meine Hand
Nach einem Schiff aus.
Mit der bloßen Faust versuche ich,
Nach seinem Segel zu greifen.
Anfangs fing ich
Verschiedene Fahrzeuge, die sich
Am Horizont zeigten.
Ich fange Forellen so.
Doch der Monsun sah mir
Auf die Finger
Und ließ sie entweichen,
Oder Ruder und Kompaß
Brachen. Man muß
Mit Schiffen zart umgehen.
Darum rief ich ihnen Namen nach.
Sie lauteten immer
Wie meiner.

Grew out of hips,
Even statues
Fired at her.
Death was put
Into everyman's hands.

She flees past, lost in herself.

At the corner the black brigand
Lies in wait for her....
Violence, with rigid metal
In his fists.

Karl Krolow

ROBINSON CRUSOE

Again and again my hand
Reaches out for a ship.
With my bare fist I try
To seize a sail.
In the beginning I caught
Several boats that
Showed up on the horizon.
I catch trout like that.
But the monsoon
Kept a strict eye on me
And let them escape,
Or rudders and compass broke.
You must be gentle,
Gentle with ships,
Therefore I call them by their names.
They were always
Like my own.

Jetzt lebe ich nur noch
In Gesellschaft mit dem Ungehorsam
Einiger Worte.

Karl Krolow

LIEBESGEDICHT

Betrügerin der Zeit! Betrügerin des Mittags,
Den ich aus feuchten Dickichten mir fische:
Wolke aus leisen Worten, leichten Silben . . . .

Das Licht schmilzt hinter deiner Schulterhöhlung,
Und aus den blauen Balsamblumen zuckt der Vogelschatten
    der Ewigkeit.
Ich folge ihm mit meinen Augen, bis er vergeht
im Abgrund deiner Nähe,
Folge den hellen Linien der Häuser
Hinterm Horizont der Stille,
Indes dem kleinen Dunkel der gekrümmten Hand
Der Kolibri der Freude mir entschlüpft
Und zwitschernd badet tief im Wasserblau der Luft.

Karl Krolow

NACH UND NACH

Nach und nach fiel sie
In die Hände seiner Worte.
Die Bäume auf dem Wege zu ihm
Waren rasch verblüht,
Die Gebüsche zerbrochen, in denen
Ihre Zärtlichkeit die Wange
An seinem Gesicht rieb.

Now I live only
In the company of a few
Disobedient words.

Karl Krolow

LOVE POEM

Beguiler of time! Beguiler of the noon
That I pluck from the damp jungles:
Cloud of soft words, floating syllables . . . .

The light melts behind the hollow of your shoulder,
The bird shadow of eternity flashes
        from the blue balsam blossoms.
I follow it with my eyes till it dissolves
In the abyss of your nearness,
Follow the bright line of houses
Behind the still horizon,
While the hummingbird of joy slips
From the small darkness of my curved hand
And bathes, twittering, deep in the water-blue of air.

Karl Krolow

BY AND BY

By and by she fell
Into the hands of his words.
The trees on the road to him
Soon ceased flowering,
The bushes withered
Where her tenderness had rubbed her cheek
Against his face.

Sie war nun in seiner Gewalt.
Wie zwischen großen Hunden,
Die jedem Fremden
Nach dem Leben trachten.
Langsam verging sie, umstellt
Von Dolchen des Gesprächs,
Das er mit ihr führte.
Sie hatte keinen Willen mehr,
Wenn der Schatten seines Bartes
Unter dem Mond auftauchte
Und seine Stimme befahl,
Ihm zu folgen . . . .

Christine Lavant

Am Fensterblech läutet der Abendregen.
Mein Teppich aus braunem Packpapier
ist voll von ermüdeten Faltern.
Daß ich nur keinen zerknie in Gottes Namen!
Mein Augenlicht ist ja schon schwach geworden
in den letzten bitteren Wochen.
Was werden wir beten, Herz, solange es läutet?
Zuerst für die Seelen im Fegefeuer,
dann für alle, die am Verzweifeln sind:
Zuchthäusler, Krebskranke und Tuberkulose.
Nicht die gefangenen Tiere vergessen,
die eingehn an Heimweh und Entsetzen!
Aber wir müssen noch weiterknien
für die lange Reihe der geistig Verwirrten
auf den gläsernen Stufen der Schwermut,
bis hinab zum höllischen Irrsinn.
Ist das überstanden, dann helfe uns Gott,

She was now in his power
As if between big hounds
That threaten
The life of every stranger.
Slowly she perished, trapped
By daggers of the talk
He carried on with her.
She no longer had a will of her own
When the shadow of his beard
Appeared under the moon
And his voice ordered her
To follow him . . . .

Christine Lavant

ORISON

Evening rain tolls on the window ledge.
My carpet of brown packing paper
is crowded with tired butterflies.
In God's holy name, I must not kneel on one of them!
My eyesight has become so poor
in the last bitter weeks.
What shall we pray for, heart, while the rain tolls?
First for the souls in purgatory,
then for all those who are near despair:
prisoners, people dying of cancer and t. b.
not forgetting trapped animals
perishing of homesickness and fright!
But we must still go on kneeling
for the long row of those with troubled minds
upon the glassy steps of hopelessness,
down to hellish madness.
This done, then may God grant us

daß uns einfällt jeder gewesene Freund,
jeder Wohltäter auch, denn ohne sie wären wir jetzt
mitten im Regen und hätten kein Dach überm Kopf,
nur Elend außen und innen.

Christine Lavant

Im hohlen Kerne des Wirbelsturms
heil und geborgen schaut meine Seele
ihren entwurzelten Innbildern nach
und der Flucht aller Zukunft.
Verschleudert wurde die Wohnung der Welt
und vom Himmel fallen die Engelsschwärme
ein in die Herzen der Menschen
und stiften dort Schrecken.
Ich habe meines nicht ausgelöst.
Es kreuzt unterm brennenden Segel
durch überzähliges Unheil hindurch
verfolgt von einem entschlossenen Engel
und den Schrecken der Heimkehr.

Christine Lavant

aus DIE BETTLERSCHALE

Wieder brach er bei dem Nachbar ein,
und ich hatte Tür und Fenster offen,
meine Augen waren vollgesoffen
wie zwei Schwämme vom Verlassensein.

that we remember every former friend,
every benefactor too, for without them
we would be out in the rain now
and have no roof over our head,
only misery outside and in us.

Christine Lavant

MY SOUL, SOUND AND SECURE

My soul, sound and secure
in the eye of the hurricane,
looks at her uprooted sisters
and at the withdrawal of all future.
The dwelling of the world is squandered,
swarms of angels are tumbling from heaven
into the hearts of man,
causing terror there.
I did not redeem my own heart.
It is cruising under burning sails
across overpowering evil
pursued by a determined angel
and the terrors of homecoming.

Christine Lavant

MY LONELINESS

Again he broke into my neighbor's house
though I threw doors and windows open wide;
my eyes are drowning in a bitter tide,
two sponges, soaked with loneliness.

Dumm verknäulte sich in meinem Mund
Schluchzen, Bitten und verbohrtes Drohen,
während drüben schon die Hühner flohen
samt der Katze und dem alten Hund.

Doch er kam nicht, nahm sich wieder nur
einen, der noch gerne leben wollte,
und die Monduhr, die verrückte, rollte
meine Stunde rasch aus seiner Spur.

Bitter trocknen meine Augen ein,
bitter rennt der Schlaftrunk durch die Kehle,
bitter bet' ich für die arme Seele
und zerkaue mein Verlassensein.

Christine Lavant

Wenn du mich einläßt bevor deine Hähne erwachen,
will ich dienen für dich in dem knöchernen Haus,
will die Herztrommel schlagen, den Atem dir schöpfen
und dreimal die geistliche Rose begießen
am Morgen, am Mittag, am Abend.

Wenn du mich einläßt bevor meine Augen verbrennen,
schmelze ich drinnen für dich dein Spiegelbild frei
und mach es zum König über die Engel
und schlage es Gott als sein Ebenbild vor,
voll Glaube, voll Hoffnung, voll Liebe.

Wenn du mich einläßt bevor mich die Kräfte verlassen,
köpfe ich neunmal für dich mit der Schlange den Tod,
grab die Gramwurzel aus und esse sie selbst
und hole dir dann aus dem Sonnengeflecht
das Brot, den Wein und die Taube.

Begging, stubborn threatening, and weeping,
knit stupidly together in my mouth,
while the chickens fled my neighbor's house,
the cat, and even the old dog, were leaving.

But to me death did not come. No, his prey
was one who wanted very much to go on living,
and soon the crazy moon-clock will have driven
my own hour from his path.

My swollen eyes dry up in bitterness.
My sleeping draught tastes bitter in my mouth,
full of bitterness I pray for his poor soul,
chewing on my loneliness.

Christine Lavant

IF YOU LET ME IN

If you let me in before your cocks awake
I will serve for you in the house of bones,
beat your heart's drum, draw your breath,
water three times the sacred rose
at dawn, at noon, and at evening.

If you let me in before my eyes are burnt,
I will thaw your likeness in there
and crown it a king over the angels
and present it to God as His image,
full of faith, full of hope, full of love.

If you let me in before my strength fails me,
nine times will I behead death with the serpent for you,
dig out the root of grief and eat it myself
and bring you then from the solar system
bread, wine, and the dove.

Christine Busta

BEGEGNUNG AUF EINER AUTOBAHN

Führ deinen Gaul nach Tarquinia, kindischer Fuhrmann!
Dort in den Tomben ist noch die Zeit des Menschen,
gehört der Himmel den Vögeln, das Meer den Fischen,
die Erde den Stieren und dem herrlichen Pferd.
Hier die Zeit ist für den Wahn von Insekten.

Oder bist du verkleidet auf heimliche Kundschaft
hergesandt von den Tänzern und Flötenspielern
aus der Tomba ins Jahrhundert des Motors?
Dann kehr um, solange der Ton der Toten
dich noch feit vor den Schwärmen mänadischer Käfer
und dem Zorn der apokalyptischen Horniß.

Fahr hinab in die versunkenen Städte
frommer Vorzeit und hüte die schönen Bilder,
bis die goldene Tuba des Jüngsten Tages
dich ans Licht ruft auf einem roten etruskischen Roß.

Christine Busta

JAHRESZEITEN

Und Nacht für Nacht fiel Schnee vor meinem Fenster,
Er fiel so leise wie verschwiegne Trauer.
Am Morgen war mein Garten ganz verschneit.

Ich weiß nicht, wo du schliefst. Gewiß war Frühling
In fremden Gärten. Alle wollen blühen.
Die Liebe lebt vom Wunder, nicht vom Recht.

Christine Busta

ENCOUNTER ON A THRUWAY

Lead your nag to Tarquinia, simple driver!
There in the tombs the Time of Man still rules,
there the sky belongs to the birds, the sea to the fish,
the earth to the steer and the marvelous horse.
Time here belongs to the madness of insects.

Or are you sent out as a scout in disguise
from the Etruscan tomb by dancers and players
into our century of the machine?
Then turn back as long as the tune of the dead
still shields you from the swarms of maenad beetles,
and the rage of apocalyptic hornets.

Descend to the buried cities
of pious antiquity and guard the fair pictures
till the golden trumpet of doomsday
calls you forth on a red Etruscan horse.

Christine Busta

SEASONS

Night after night snow fell outside my windows,
It came as quietly as secret sorrow;
At dawn my garden was deep under snow.

I wish I knew where you are sleeping. Spring reigns,
I know, in other gardens, and they all will bloom.
Love lives by magic only, not by right.

Für jede Stunde, die du fern warst, hob ich
Dir eine Flocke auf. Ich find sie nimmer.
Nun wird es wohl vor fremden Fenstern schnei'n.

Rainer Brambach

HUNDSTAGE

Allmählich versiegen die Brunnen
Die herrenlosen Hunde suchen nach Wasser
Der Gewürzhändler nickt ein in seinem Gewölbe
Niemand kauft Pfeffer
Draußen bewegt der Scherenschleifer lässig sein Rad
Er verscheucht lautlos die Hunde
Er beobachtet den Händler
Er wartet ab
Es ist die Zeit der geschärften Klingen.

Rainer Brambach

PAUL

Neunzehnhundertsiebzehn
an einem Tag unter Null geboren,

rannte er wild über den Kinderspielplatz,
fiel, und rannte weiter,

den Ball werfend über den Schulhof,
fiel, und rannte weiter,

I saved a snowflake for each single hour
You were away, and now I cannot find them.
And snow will fall at other windows now.

Rainer Brambach

DOG DAYS

Little by little the wells are drying up
Stray dogs are trying to find water
The spice dealer is nodding off in his vault
Nobody buys pepper
Outside the scissor grinder
Lazily turns his wheel
Silently he drives off the dogs
He watches the spice dealer
He waits
It is the time of sharpened blades.

Rainer Brambach

PAUL

Nineteen hundred and seventeen
born on a day below zero,

wildly he ran across the playground,
fell down, and ran on,

threw the ball across the schoolyard,
fell down, and ran on,

das Gewehr im Arm über das Übungsgelände,
fiel, und rannte weiter,

an einem Tag unter Null
in ein russisches Sperrfeuer

und fiel.

Johannes Bobrowski

WAGENFAHRT

Schöner Mond von Mariampol! Auf deinem
strohernen Rand, mein Städtchen,
hinter den Buden
kommt er herauf,
schwer, und hängt ein wenig
nach unten durch. So geht der
Pferdehändler, er kauft
seiner Mutter ein Fransentuch.

Abends
spät
sangen die beiden. Wir fuhren
über den Fluß nach Haus,
an der Fähre mit Ruf und Zuruf
ging Gerede wie Wasser
leicht—und wir hörten ihn lang
über der Stadt,
droben in Türmen, hörten
den jüdischen Mond. Der ist
wie im Gartenwinkel das kleine
Kraut aus Tränen und Küssen,
Raute, unsere Mädchen
brechen es ab.

a gun in his arm, across the training ground,
fell down, and ran on,

on a day below zero
into a Russian barrage

and fell.

Johannes Bobrowski

HOME RIDE

Fair moon of Mariampol! Rising.
My little town, behind your strawy edges,
behind your shacks,
the moon is rising, heavily,
sagging a little at her lower edge.
The horse dealer walks like that.
He bought a fringed scarf
for his mother.

In the evening
late
the two were singing. We drove home
across the river; calling and talking
went back and forth,
light, like water
—and for a long time
we heard over the city
up there in the steeples, heard
the Jewish moon.
She is like the small herb
made of tears and kisses,
rue, our girls pick it
in the corner of their gardens.

. . . . .

Joneleit, komm, verlier dein
Tuch nicht. Die Alten schlafen.
Ausgesungen wieder
ist eine Nacht.

Johannes Bobrowski

STEPPE

Einer war,
der sang in den Abend. Draußen
schwer die Ebene,
baumlos, um niedres Gewächs
brennend der Sand—
da hielten die Wolken dunkel,
und ein Mond hing herab.
An dem Wasserloch falb
die Herde. Einer, braunbärtig,
kam, er trieb die Rinder
fort. Im Fenster der andere
sang.

Dörfer,
wie will ich leben
noch? In der Ferne weiß ich
endlos entrinnender Himmel
Glanz. Den Jungen, der sang,
und den Hüter mit hellen
Augen hörte ich reden
an der Straße, ich stand,
im Rücken das Dorf.

. . . . .

Joneleit, come, do not lose
the scarf. The old are sleeping.
We sang away
another night.

Johannes Bobrowski

STEPPE

A boy, singing
in the evening. Outside
the plain, heavy,
treeless; sand burning
around the low bushes—
then the clouds halted, darkly,
and a moon was drooping.
A drove of cattle, cream-colored
at the water hole. A man,
brown-bearded, came and drove away
the cattle. In the window
the boy was still singing.

Villages,
how shall I live, now?
In the distance I know
the glow of endlessly fleeing skies.
I hear the boy who sang and
the light-eyed herdsman talking
in the street. I am standing still,
the village at my back.

Hans Bender

OKTOBERENDE

Ins grüne Vogellachen
tropft der Regen seine Trauer.
Dein Sonnenauge
überm Garten
schwärzt der Frost.
Aufs Pflaster stürzten
eure braunen Zärtlichkeiten.
Hände,
rot vom Blut des Sommers,
spült der Bach
durch eisigen Granit.

Hans Bender

DER JUNGE SOLDAT

als er vom Begräbnis seiner sieben
Kameraden zur Front zurückging

In die Blumen ihrer Haare
Rieselte die listge Erde.
Auf die Särge ihrer Brust
Klopften unsre stummen Würfe.
Sieben gelbe, warme Gräber
Trocknen in der Julisonne.

Wiesenweg durch heißen Mohn.
Wälderweg durch kalte Tannen.
Weg, der blind im Sumpf erstickt.
Ungewisser Minenweg—
Dann vorbei an hellen Hütten.
Vorhangfalten, Fensterglas.

Hans Bender

END OF OCTOBER

Rain drips its lament
into a green bird's laughter.
Your sun eye
over the garden
is blackened by frost.
Your brown tenderness
tumbles down to the pavement.
Hands,
red with summer's blood,
are floating on the brook
between chilly granite rocks.

Hans Bender

YOUNG SOLDIER

*Returning to the front after the funeral of his
seven friends*

On their soft, their flowery hair
Cunning earth has drifted, piled.
Upon their chests, so much like coffins,
Earth fell, thudding, from our hands.
Seven warm clay-yellow graves
Are drying in the summer sun.

Meadow road through flaming poppies.
Forest road through chilly pine grove.
Road that blindly ends in bog.
Road that winds through treacherous mine field—
Then past brightly painted huts,
Pleated curtains, windowpanes.

Beerentrauben in den Gärten.
Rosenstrauß, Gladiolengarbe.
Brunnen dran der Eimer schwappt
Vor den Zäunen steife Mädchen.
In die Löcher der Pupillen
Haß, vom Schreck hineingebohrt.

Trauer durch den Sommer tragen.
Schultergurt und rauhes Tuch.
Handgranate, Spaten, Helm,
Das Gewehr und die Geschosse.
Messer, eingekerbt die Rille,
Für das Blut der stumpfen Rücken.

Sieben fette Krähen wehen
Aus den Ästen roter Föhren.
Sieben schwarze Federn fallen
In die Raupenspur des Tanks.

Hans Bender

GEMEINSAM

Das Messer teilt unser Brot
in gleiche Stücke.
Wo deine Lippen am Glas lagen,
trink ich den zweiten Schluck.
Geh in meinen Schuhen!
Wenn der Winter kommt,
wärmt mich dein Mantel.
Wir weinen aus einem Auge,
schließen am Abend die Tür,
allein zu sein. Im Schlaf
greifen deine Träume in meine.

Berry clusters in the gardens.
Rose bush, and gladioli sheaf.
Wells where wooden pails are swaying.
At the fences rigid girls,
Hatred staring from their eyes,
Drilled by fright, blank holes: their pupils.

Carrying woe through summer days.
Shoulder straps, coarse uniform,
Hand grenades, a spade, a helmet,
And the gun, the ammunition.
Knife, a groove carved in the handle,
For the blood of apathetic backs.

Seven well-fed crows drift down
From the boughs of reddish fir trees.
Seven coal-black feathers drop
Into the rough tracks of tanks.

Hans Bender

TOGETHER

A knife cuts our bread
into identical pieces.
I drink
where your lips touched the glass.
Walk in my shoes!
Your coat will warm me
when winter comes.
We weep with the same eye.
In the evening we close the door
to be alone. In our sleep
your dreams reach out into
my dreams.

Paul Celan

SCHLAF UND SPEISE

Der Hauch der Nacht ist dein Laken, die Finsternis legt sich
      zu dir.
Sie rührt dich an Knöchel und Schläfe, sie weckt dich zu
      Leben und Schlaf,
Sie spürt dich im Wort auf, im Wunsch, im Gedanken,
sie schläft bei jedem von ihnen, sie lockt dich hervor.
Sie kämmt dir das Salz aus den Wimpern und tischt es
      dir auf,
sie lauscht deinen Stunden den Sand ab und setzt ihn dir
      vor.
Und was sie als Rose war, Schatten und Wasser,
schenkt sie dir ein.

Paul Celan

TODESFUGE

Schwarze Milch der Frühe wir trinken sie abends
wir trinken sie mittags und morgens wir trinken
      sie nachts
wir trinken und trinken
wir schaufeln ein Grab in den Lüften da liegt man
      nicht eng
Ein Mann wohnt im Haus der spielt mit den
      Schlangen der schreibt
der schreibt wenn es dunkelt nach Deutschland
      dein goldenes Haar Margarete
er schreibt es und tritt vor das Haus und es blitzen
      die Sterne er pfeift seine Rüden herbei
er pfeift seine Juden hervor läßt schaufeln ein
      Grab in der Erde
er befiehlt uns spielt auf nun zum Tanz

Paul Celan

SLEEP AND FOOD

The breath of night is your sheet, darkness lies down
  at your side.
It touches your ankle and brow, awakes you to
  life and to sleep.
It ferrets your self out in words, in wish and in thought,
sleeping with each of them it lures you out to the open.
It combs the salt from your lashes and serves it to you,
listens for sand in your hours, and puts it before you.
And what it once was—as rose, as shadow, as water—
that it pours out for you.

Paul Celan

FUGUE OF DEATH

Dark milk of dawn we drink it in the evening
we drink it at noon in the morning we drink it
  at night
we drink and we drink
we are digging a grave in the clouds where we will
  not be crowded
In the house lives a man who plays with vipers
  who writes
who writes when the night falls to Germany
  your golden hair Margareta
he writes it and steps out of doors the stars glitter there
  and he calls to his hounds hey come here
he calls to his jews come here come on dig a grave
  in the ground
he commands us to strike up for a dance

Schwarze Milch der Frühe wir trinken dich nachts
wir trinken dich morgens und mittags wir trinken
    dich abends
wir trinken und trinken
Ein Mann wohnt im Haus der spielt mit den
    Schlangen der schreibt
der schreibt wenn es dunkelt nach Deutschland
    dein goldenes Haar Margarete
Dein aschenes Haar Sulamith wir schaufeln ein Grab
    in den Lüften da liegt man nicht eng

Er ruft stecht tiefer ins Erdreich ihr einen ihr
    andern singet und spielt
er greift nach dem Eisen im Gurt er schwingts seine
    Augen sind blau
stecht tiefer die Spaten ihr einen ihr andern
    spielt weiter zum Tanz auf

Schwarze Milch der Frühe wir trinken dich nachts
wir trinken dich mittags und morgens wir trinken
    dich abends
wir trinken und trinken
ein Mann wohnt im Haus dein goldenes Haar
    Margarete
dein aschenes Haar Sulamith er spielt mit den
    Schlangen

Er ruft spielt süßer den Tod der Tod ist ein Meister
    aus Deutschland
er ruft streicht dunkler die Geigen dann steigt ihr
    als Rauch in die Luft
dann habt ihr ein Grab in den Wolken da liegt
    man nicht eng

Schwarze Milch der Frühe wir trinken dich nachts
wir trinken dich mittags der Tod ist ein Meister
    aus Deutschland

Dark milk of dawn   we drink it at night
we drink it in the morning   at noon   we drink it
        in the evening
we drink and we drink
In the house lives a man who plays with vipers
        who writes
who writes when the night falls   to Germany
        your golden hair   Margareta
Your ashen hair   Sulamith   we are digging a grave
        in the clouds where we will not be crowded

He calls   dig the ground deeper   you here
        and you there play the fiddle and sing
he clutches the gun in his belt   he waves it
        how blue are his eyes
drive the spade deeper   you here   and you there
        strike up for a dance

Dark milk of dawn   we drink it at night
we drink it at noon   in the morning   we drink it
        in the evening
we drink and we drink
in the house lives a man   your golden hair
        Margareta
your ashen hair   Sulamith   he plays with
        vipers

He calls   play the death tune sweeter   for death is
        a master from Germany
he calls   play the fiddles darker   then you'll rise
        as smoke to the sky
then you'll have a grave in the clouds where you
        won't be so crowded

Dark milk of dawn   we drink it at night
we drink it at noon   death is a master
        from Germany

wir trinken dich abends und morgens wir trinken
    und trinken
der Tod ist ein Meister aus Deutschland sein Auge
    ist blau
er trifft dich mit bleierner Kugel er trifft dich genau
ein Mann wohnt im Haus dein goldenes Haar
    Margarete
er hetzt seine Rüden auf uns er schenkt uns ein
    Grab in der Luft
er spielt mit den Schlangen und träumet der Tod
    ist ein Meister aus Deutschland
dein goldenes Haar Margarete
dein aschenes Haar Sulamith

Paul Celan

Nachts, wenn das Pendel der Liebe schwingt
zwischen Immer und Nie,
stößt dein Wort zu den Monden des Herzens
und dein gewitterhaft blaues
Aug reicht der Erde den Himmel.

Aus fernem, aus traumgeschwärztem
Hain weht uns an das Verhauchte,
und das Versäumte geht um, groß wie die Schemen der
    Zukunft.

Was sich nun senkt und hebt,
gilt dem zuinnerst Vergrabnen:
blind, wie der Blick, den wir tauschen,
küßt es die Zeit auf den Mund.

we drink it at dusk and at dawn   we drink
    and we drink
death is a master from Germany   blue
    are his eyes
he hits with a leaden bullet   he hits you precisely
in the house lives a man   your golden hair
    Margareta
he sets his lean hounds on us   he gives us
    a grave in the clouds
he plays with vipers and dreams that death
    is a master from Germany
your golden hair   Margareta
your ashen hair   Sulamith

Paul Celan

AT NIGHT

At night when the pendulum of love
swings between forever and never,
your word joins the moon of the heart
and your thunder-blue eyes
offer the sky to the earth.

From the distant, from the dream-darkened
grove a faraway breeze drifts toward us,
and deeds, not done, haunt us, large like phantoms
    of the future.

What is now rising and sinking
concerns what is buried in our heart's deepest core:
blind, like the gaze we exchange,
it kisses time on her lips.

Alfred Gong

DIE GRENZE

Die andere Seite ist ein Spiegel dieser unserer:
die gleichen Birken und die gleiche Nacht.
Seltsam: der Mond
strahlt groß und wohnt auf jener Seite....
Die drüben—ich kannte welche früher
als die andere Seite noch keine andere Seite war—
die drüben sprechen ganz die gleiche Sprache;
jetzt aber schweigen sie
und auch wir schweigen.
Verschiedenes Schweigen.

Wir, hier auf Wache,
in dieser Nacht, zwischen den Birken,
wir sprechen nicht mal unter uns.
Ganz Ohr sind wir, gezückt
der Herzen Klopfen zu erspähen
jener, die (weiß nicht warum) hinüber wollen,
hinüber auf die Seite
wo der Mond strahlt groß und wartet.

Solch eine Nacht wär gut für stille Träume,
im Gras die Glieder und das Aug im Sternengarten,
ja, eine Nacht ein Mädchen fest an sich zu drücken
und nicht dies kalte Automatgewehr.
Seltsam.
Seltsam im Mond der Tau
an jenen Knospen des Stacheldrahts....

—Horch!...Hast du es auch gehört?
—Wer wird es wagen bei solch großem Mond...
Der Wind ist's nur, verspielt in Birkenwipfeln,
vielleicht ein Tier der Nacht,

Alfred Gong

IRON CURTAIN

The other side is a mirror of ours:
The same birches and the same night.
Strange: the moon
shines large and waits on that side....
People over there—I knew some, once,
when the other side was not yet another side—
speak the same language;
but they are silent now
and we are silent too.
A different silence.

We, here on guard
in this night under the birches,
we do not talk even to each other.
We are all ears, intent
to catch the pounding of the hearts
of those who (I don't know why) want to cross over,
over to the side
where the moon shines large and waits.

Such a night is good for quiet dreams,
limbs in the grass, eyes in the garden of stars,
yes, a night to hold a girl close
and not this cold gun.
Strange.
Strange the dew in moonlight
on buds of barbed wire....

—Listen!...Did you hear it too?
—Who would dare in this full moon—
It's only the wind, playful in the birch boughs,
maybe a creature of the night,

ein Vogel, der aus seinen Träumen flattert,
Der Wind ein Tier der Nacht...

.....

Zu spät war es als wir das Flüchtlingspaar gewahrten:
sie liefen auf der anderen Seite
im Schauer klaren Silberlichtes.
Und blieben stehn.
Die Arme weit geöffnet, zwei Kreuzen gleich.
Und sahen sich noch einmal um,
bevor sie ineinander sanken
und später in den Tau.

Wie seltsam, seltsam.
Man möchte in den Mond die Ladung feuern
und still nachhause gehn.

Alfred Gong

MARS

September—schrieben die Buchen.
Im Park abecete der Lehrer,
als plötzlich auftrat der Fremde
klirrend.
Weil der Lehrer erbleichte,
johlten die Kinder.

Mars ging durch die Stadt
und multiplizierte die Fahnen,
er nahm den Trinkspruch entgegen.
(Besonders gefiel ihm das Wörtchen „gerecht")
Ein Friseur stutzte ihn unentgeltlich,
unentgeltlich beschlug ihn ein Schmied.

a bird, fluttering from its dreams.
The wind a creature of night....

.....

Too late we noticed the fugitives:
running on the other side
in a shower of clear silver light.
And stood still.
Arms wide open, resembling two crosses,
and looked around once more
before they sank against each other,
and later into the dew.

How strange, strange.
You feel like firing your rounds at the moon
and silently going home.

Alfred Gong

MARS

September—the beech trees wrote.
In the park the teacher a-b-c'ed
when suddenly the stranger appeared,
clanking.
Because the teacher grew pale,
the children shrieked.

Mars walked through the city
multiplying the flags;
he accepted the toast.
(He especially liked the little word "just")
A barber trimmed him for nothing,
for nothing a smith shod him.

Mars nahm im Rathaus Quartier:
er schwärmte für Türme
und schätzte Karteien besonders.
Er sammelte Lumpen- und Alteisensammler
und schlug sie zum Ritter und Rat.
In der Falte seines Rockes verborgen
harrte der Heuschreck.

Strengste Verdunklung—befahl er
und knirschte den Mond an,
als jener seinen Befehl
ab und zu nur befolgte.

Alfred Gong

DIE FLIEGENDE ARCHE

> „Toda la noche oyeron pasar pájaros"
>
> (Columbus, *Tagebuch*)

„Man hörte die ganze Nacht Vögel vorüberziehen":
Myriaden, in Schwärmen, durchrauschten den Traum
und verwischten Kassiopeia. Auf ihren Warten
die Wächter drehen die Rohre nach Nord und Nadir,
nach Süd und Zenit, Deutung nicht wissend, noch Rat.

Was—in dieser Julinacht—ruft sie aus Düne und Delta?
Wer befiehlt der Ornis aufzubrechen klagend
aus Hain und aus Urwald?, aufzuflattern im Bauer
verzweifelt, zu ungewöhnlicher Stunde?
Was funkt ihr Instinkt? Was weiß diese nächtliche Flotte?

Mars took quarters in the city hall,
he was enthusiastic about towers
and above all, he appreciated card indexes.
He collected ragpickers and bums,
and made them knight and adviser.
Hidden in a fold of his garment
the locust lurked.

"Strictest blackout!" he commanded
and gnashed his teeth at the moon
when she followed his order
only now and then.

Alfred Gong

THE FLYING ARK

> "Toda la noche oyeron pasar pájaros"
>
> (*Diary of Columbus*)

"All night long we heard birds flying past":
Millions, in swarms, rustled through the dream
and blurred Cassiopeia. The watchmen on the roofs
turn their telescopes to the north, to the nadir,
to the south and the zenith, knowing no explanation,
      no advice.

What, in this night of July, calls them from delta and dune?
Who orders the ornis to set out, lamenting,
from grove and from jungle—to flutter, desperate,
in their cages at this unusual hour?
What does their instinct report? What does this
      nightly fleet know?

Die Jet-Clipper steigen heute nicht auf.
(Alle Radare flimmern konfus)
Die Flieger betrinken sich still oder gehen zu Bett.

Seht, auf den Türmen bestaunen die Seher
in den Kegeln aus Licht nie Geahntes:
Den Kormoran, tragend im Schnabel zärtlich die Otter—
den Roten Milan mit einem stillen Hasen als Fracht—
zwei Kaiseradler, jeder ein menschliches Junges
sorgfältig führend mit der Kraft seiner Krallen—
und den Greif, den man längst ausgelöscht wußte,
vorüberdröhnend mit einem dankbaren Löwen.

Was steht unseren Breiten bevor?
Was erwartet uns—ohne Flügel?
Wir werden es morgen erfahren,
wenn es wieder zu spät.

Alfred Gong

ERKENNTNIS

Als es auf die Stadt,
auf die Stadt der hundert Kirchen
Feuer und Schwefel regnete:
verkohlte der Heiland aus Holz
zerrann der Heiland aus Wachs
schmolz der Heiland aus Gold
zerbrach der Heiland aus Stein.

Und als es still wurde,
still in der Stadt der tausend Ruinen,
meinte einer:

The jet planes do not take off today.
(The radars flicker confusingly.)
The pilots get quietly drunk or go to sleep.

Behold! Those seers on towers gaze astounded
at this never-imagined sight in the cone of light:
The cormorant tenderly carrying an otter in its beak—
the red falcon with a quiet rabbit as its burden—
two golden eagles, each carefully transporting
a human baby in its strong talons—
And the griffin, long since known to be extinct,
thundering past with a grateful lion.

What is threatening us in our latitude?
What will happen to us—to us without wings?
We shall know it tomorrow
when, once more, it will be too late.

Alfred Gong

COGNITION

When it rained fire and brimstone
upon the city,
upon the city of a hundred churches,
the wooden Saviour was charred,
the waxen Saviour was dissolved,
the golden Saviour was melted,
the stone Saviour was shattered.

And when it became quiet,
quiet in the city of a thousand ruins,
somebody said:

So bleibt uns nur eins:
Ihn diesmal formen
aus Asche
aus Schwefel
aus Tränen
aus Herz und Herz und Herz.

Helmut Heissenbüttel

FENSTERINHALTE

Das Rührende des Novemberabends zum Beispiel.
Geometrie der senkrecht verstellten Hinterhauswände.
Waschleinenphysiognomie des Balkons.
Das Hingetuschte des Himmels.
Bürsten der Schattenbäume.
Oder einfach der senkrecht fallende Ball aus Spatzenfedern.
Das Bild des ausgeschnittenen Rechtecks tröstet.
Trost der Sichtbarkeit.

Helmut Heissenbüttel

EINFACHE SÄTZE

Während ich stehe fällt der Schatten hin
Morgensonne entwirft die erste Zeichnung
Blühn ist ein tödliches Geschäft
Ich habe mich einverstanden erklärt
Ich lebe

Only one thing is left for us to do—
now we must form Him
of ashes,
of brimstone,
of tears,
of heart and heart and heart.

Helmut Heissenbüttel

CONTENTS OF WINDOWS

For example the pathetic quality of a November evening.
Geometry of backyard walls, vertically arranged.
Clotheslinephysiognomy of the balcony.
Washed drawing of the sky.
Shadowtree brushes.
Or simply the plummeting ball of sparrow feathers.
The picture in the cutout square is comforting.
Consolation of the visible.

Helmut Heissenbüttel

SIMPLE SENTENCES

While I am standing my shadow is lying at my feet
Morning sun sketches the first design
To bloom is a deadly business
I have given my consent
I live

Walter Höllerer

IM MITTAGSLICHT

Ein Rosenkäfer findet durch den Duft die Furt.
Ein Mauersegler ritzt mit Flügeln dunkles Blau.
Ein Mädchen liest in einem Buch
Die Linien ohne Furcht.

Am Halm umgrenzt sich ein Kristall.
In fernen Nebeln sirrt ein Silberstern.
Durch Adern zuckt es brennend rot:
Es ist. Ich bin.

Es wandern Masten, schwarz, in Reihn durchs Land.
Ein Flugzeug schwimmt am Wolkenrand.
Hornisse tobt, sekundenschnell, im Sand—im Kreis,
Das Licht, der Tag ist hell, ist heiß.

Kuno Raeber

BEIM ANZÜNDEN DER ZIGARETTE

Wenn du das Feuer
hinhältst der Dame, die
leicht zurückweicht, weil aus dem Wagen,
der plötzlich anhielt, der Fahrer
öffnet auf euch zu die Tür,
achtlos: trittst Du,
Kaiser, ins Kloster
und findest enttäuscht
die Rosen alle gekappt,
bis dir nach wenigen
Schritten im Teehaus der Abt

Walter Höllerer

IN THE LIGHT OF NOON

A rose beetle finds the ford across the fragrance.
A black martin cuts the dark blue with its wings.
A girl reads in a book,
Reads without fear.

A crystal shapes itself, hanging from a stalk.
A silver star whirs in far nebulae.
Burning red it flashes through my veins:
It is. I am.

And masts are wandering, black, in rows across the land.
A plane swims at the edge of clouds.
A hornet rages, lightning quick, in sand—in circles,
The light, the day is bright, is hot.

Kuno Raeber

LIGHTING A CIGARETTE

When you are offering the flame
to the lady who retreats slightly
as from the suddenly stopping car
the driver opens the door toward you,
carelessly: you enter,
O emperor, the monastery
and discover, disappointed,
that all the roses have been cut,
but after a few steps
the abbot in the tea house
silently shows you—

zeigt, schweigend, die aufging am Morgen,
allein in der Vase die Rose:
wenn du der Dame, die leicht
zurückweicht, die Zigarette anzündest.

Kuno Raeber

DER FUDSCHIJAMA

Gefühlswälder sind süß zu durchwandern,
weil sie die Tageszeit nie genau erkennen lassen,
sondern die Ränder mit dem Dämmerlappen immer
      sorgsam verwischen,
und weil nachts in den Mondlichtungen uns immer das
      gleiche Reh
aus großen nassen Augen ansieht und rührt.

Erst draußen am Abfall der Klippen,
wo nicht einmal mehr geducktes Gebüsch den
      Salzwind mildert
und wo die Nacht nackt ist im scharfen Wintergespräch
      mit dem von der Woge aufs höchste gereizten,
über den Golf laut Schnee redenden Berg Fudschijama:
da erst begreifen wir, warum wir so lange gegangen.

Margot Scharpenberg

ORTSVERÄNDERUNG

Zugvogelunrast, doch ohne
Süden und jenes
gelassene Pendel der Rückkehr.
Da wartet kein Dach.

burst into bloom this morning
alone in a vase—a rose:
as you are lighting the cigarette
for the slightly retreating lady.

Kuno Raeber

FUJIYAMA

Sweet it is to wander through woods of emotion
because they never let us sense the time of day
always carefully blurring all the edges with dawn-
     colored rags,
because at night in moon-clearings always the same doe
gazes at us with large moist eyes moving our hearts.

Only beyond, at the sheer drop of cliffs,
where not even cowering bushes gentle the salt wind,
where night is naked in sharp winter-talk with towering
     —enraged by the wave,
     snow talking loudly across the gulf—
with towering Fujiyama:
only there we know why we walked such a long way.

Margot Scharpenberg

CHANGE OF SCENERY

Restless as a migrant bird
but without a South
nor the serene pendulum of a return.
No roof is waiting.

Gnadenlos schlägt mich,
Aufbruch bestimmend,
mehr denn Zeit aus der Bahn.

Fremde hat finstere Werber,
die machten mich trunken
mit Hoffnung und ewiger Sicht.

Wo war ich gestern?
Verlassen bleiben die Städte
Trümmer und
nie mehr erreichtes Ziel.

Margot Scharpenberg

VERGEBENS

Barfuß fragt ich
die Dornenspur nach dem Weg.
Bekam eine Antwort.

Ich wüßte wohin,
könnt ich noch gehen.

Margot Scharpenberg

FLÜCHTIG

Kind auf dem Rücken,
so schlepp ich die Zeit,
hänge sie, wenn ich raste,
zwischen zwei Pfosten ins Tuch.

Something stronger than time
determines departure and throws me,
merciless, out of my groove.

The unknown has grim solicitors.
They made me drunk
with hope and eternal vision.

Where was I yesterday?
The cities, abandoned, remain
ruins. A goal
out of my reach now forever.

Margot Scharpenberg

IN VAIN

Barefooted I asked
the thorns for my way.
Received an answer.

I would know where to go
could I keep walking.

Margot Scharpenberg

FLEETING MOMENT

Child on my back—
thus I carry the time,
dangle him, while I am resting,
in a scarf between posts.

Immer mit einer Hand
rühr ich die Wiege.
Es glaubt, wir gingen, und schläft.
Sei leise, unser Betrug
will den Augenblick retten.
Schreit es, dann müssen wir gehn.

Heinz Piontek

ROMANZE VOM ABSCHIED

Okarina des Abschieds
bläst mir der heitere Herbst,
Farben von Safran und getrocknetem Blut—

ach, mit dem Rauch der Kartoffelfeuer
zieht die chimärische Dauer
hinter die Steigung des Hangs.

Was mir geliehen wurde:
wechselndes Licht an den Wänden,
Verständnis für manche Vergeblichkeit,
ein tiefer gespürter Schimmer des Laubes—
dem Unerfahrbaren geb ichs zurück.

Heinz Piontek

UNANFECHTBARES BILD

Die Vögel schwärmen
aus den Gebüschen:

Schneeschmelze von Westen.

With one hand I am constantly
stirring the cradle.
He thinks we keep going and sleeps.
Be still, our deceit
will save this moment.
When he starts screaming then we must go.

Heinz Piontek

SONG OF FAREWELL

Serene autumn plays for me
the ocarina of farewell,
colors of saffron and dried blood—

ah, with the smoke of potato-fires
permanence floats like a chimera
beyond the rise of the slope.

What was loaned to me:
changing light on walls,
understanding of many a futility,
a deeper-felt glimmer of leaves—
I give them back to the never-to-be-known.

Heinz Piontek

INCONTESTABLE IMAGE

Birds are lured
from bushes:

Thawing wind from the West.

Erlöstes Erz aus der Münze,
ergießt sich über die Stufen
feuriges Wasser.

Doch du, Figurine
mit blauer Iris,
kommst gläsern beschuht.

Harmlos mörderisch
führst du die Waffen
der Schönheit.

Alles vergeht an der
unauslöschlichen Sonne.

Du aber sinkst nicht hin.

Heinz Piontek

VERGÄNGLICHE PSALMEN

Singet Ihm ein neues Lied ... Psalm 33.3

II

Ich rühme Dich im Weidendschungel der Donau.
Ich rühme Dich.
Deinen Namen hefte ich auf die grünen Fahnen einer
      Platane.

Du wehst die Taubenrotte meiner Sehnsucht ins Licht,
Du legst Deinen Frieden auf meine erbitterten Träume
und Deine Langmut an meine entblößten Schläfen.

Ich bilde aus Deinem Atem Gedanken, die Dich loben.

Fiery water,
freed metal from coins,
cascading down the stairs.

But you, figurine
with blue iris,
you come in shoes of glass.

Harmlessly murderous,
you wield the weapons
of beauty.

Everything melts
in the ineffaceable sun.

But you do not yield.

Heinz Piontek

SHORT-LIVED PSALMS

Sing unto Him a new song... Psalm 33.3

II

I praise Thee in the willow jungles of the Danube.
I praise Thee.
I fasten Thy name upon the green flags of a plane tree.

Thou wavest the dove flock of my longing into light,
Thou layest Thy peace on my embittered dreams,
and Thy forbearance upon my defenseless forehead.

From Thy breath I form thoughts that praise Thee.

IV

Lange schweigst Du in den vier Wänden der Einsamkeit.
Die Lesekammer staut den Geruch der Druckfarben,
        welker Äpfel,
aus dem Staubflaum der Lampenglocke
seilt sich die Spinne ins Leere.

Ich zerreiße die Photographie des letzten Sommers.
Aus Teichgrün und Lichtschaum blies ich das Glas
        gebrechlicher Träumereien,
bei gelbem Lavabel und einem Wasserglas voll Absinth
schloß ich leichtfertig Frieden.

Der halbblaute Terror durch überheizte Baracken,
Verhöre um Mitternacht, Erschoßne
        in hallenden Kellern—
das alles war zu vergessen.

Doch jetzt belagert es mich, murmelnd und tückisch.
Ich schreibe Dein Schweigen in die Protokolle meiner
        Schwermut.

XIII

Du segnest mich mit Leid und füllst meine Taschen mit
        tauben Früchten,
aber ich hoffe auf Dich.
Wo Du die Erde grünen läßt zwischen den Brandmauern
        des Elends
und über den Quadern gesprengter Brücken,
wächst mir ewig Deine Barmherzigkeit zu.

Du heftest die Medaille der Sonne an geplatzte Scheiben,
Du sitzt unter den Bettlern, wenn sie des Nachts auf den
        Promenaden rauchen und frieren,
in den Irrenhäusern löschst Du das Licht und entzündest
        die schwarze Fackel des Schlafs.

IV

A long time hast Thou been silent in the four walls
     of loneliness.
The reading chamber holds the smell of printer's ink,
     of shriveled apples,
a spider spins its thread into emptiness
from the fluffy dust of the lampshade.

I tear up the pictures of last summer.
Out of pond-green and light-foam I blew the glass
     of brittle dreams,
with yellow rayon and a water glass of absinthe
I made an insincere peace.

Muffled terror through overheated barracks,
trial hearings at midnight, men murdered
     in resounding cellars—
all that had to be forgotten.

But now it lays siege to me, murmuring and vicious.
I am writing Thy silence into the records of my sadness.

XIII

Thou blessest me with sorrow and fillest my pockets with
     barren fruit,
but in Thee do I put my trust.
Wherever Thou lettest the earth grow green between the
     burnt walls of misery
and over the hewn stones of shattered bridges,
there Thy mercy is, forever, upon me.

Thou placest medals of sunshine on cracked panes,
At night Thou sittest among beggars in the avenues as they
     smoke and shiver,
in the asylums Thou puttest out the light and kindlest
     the dark torch of sleep.

Was Du mir zumißt, ist das Erträgliche.
Ich fürchte mich vor einer Last, die ich nicht abschütteln
        werde.
Ich gehe der Finsternis entgegen, mit kleinen Schritten.

Hans Rudolf Hilty

LORELEI

Zu Bacharach am Rheine
harrt Lorelei mit blaugrünen Modigliani-Mandeln in den
        Augenhöhlen:
nachgeborener Mond eines zerborstenen Planeten,
Fremdlingin unter den Sonntagsfischern der Liebe,
die nicht wissen, was soll das bedeuten.

Ganz im Gegensatz zu diesen
hat längst sie begriffen, daß Demokratie,
Relativitätstheorie und Teilbarkeit des Atoms
eine neue Weltschau konstituieren:
Kurz geschoren hat sie ihr lockendes Mondhaar.

Und was sie jetzt kämmt noch, sitzend
zu Bacharach am Rheine
im Abendgeleucht auf dem Felsen des Bewußtseins,
ist bloß die reine Imagination ihres Haares.

Manchmal aber, trotzdem, verfängt sich darin die Angel
eines der wohlgenährten Sonntagsfischer der Liebe,
die nicht wissen, was soll das bedeuten,
und er stürzt vornüber
—daß ich so traurig bin—
in die Stromschnellen ihrer blaugrünen Modigliani-Augen.

What Thou metest out to me is bearable.
I am afraid of a burden that I shall not cast off.
I walk toward darkness, with small steps.

Hans Rudolf Hilty

LORELEI

At Bacharach on the Rhine, Lorelei is lingering.
blue-green Modigliani-almonds in her eye sockets:
posthumous moon of a cracked planet,
stranger among amateur fishers of love,
"who know not whence comes the feeling."

Quite in contrast to these men
she realized, long since, that democracy,
the theory of relativity, and the divisibility of the atom
constitute a new philosophy:
she wears her enticing moon-hair bobbed.

And what she is combing now,
sitting at Bacharach on the Rhine
on the rock of consciousness in the evening glow,
is only the sheer image of her hair.

Sometimes though, in spite of our modern times, the hook
of a well-fed Sunday fisherman of love becomes
            entangled in it,
"who knows not whence comes the feeling"
and he falls headlong
—*"oh sadness in my heart"*—
into the rapids of her blue-green Modigliani eyes.

Hans Rudolf Hilty

SOMMER-FRAGMENT

Zu tief bin ich gesunken
in die Schlingpflanzen der Müdigkeit,
in die heimlichen Krater der Schwermut
weit unterm lockenden Spiegel.

Da steigen keine Blasen mehr auf
als lichternde Bälle.

Und weiß doch: Oben ist ein Himmel,
sommerlich blau und flirrend vor Fülle des Lichts,
und schlägt eine Amsel früh im Geäst
des dunkel blutenden Flieders, den ich so heiß
geliebt.

Um mich die flachen Leiber der Fische.
Und das ziehende Rieseln des Sands.

Oliver Behnssen

KOEXISTENZ

Ein Atoll voller Tauben,
Lachtauben,
Atomtauben,
voll lachender Atomtauben,
Atomlachtauben,
Friedenstauben,
lachender Atomfriedenstauben,
voll Atomlachfriedenstauben,

Hans Rudolf Hilty

SUMMER-FRAGMENT

I sank too deep
into the drift-weed of tiredness,
into the secret craters of gloom
deep under the beckoning mirror.

There are no more bubbles rising
like flickering balls.

Yet I know: there above is a sky,
summery blue and glittering with abundance of light,
and a thrush trills, early, in the boughs
of dark-bleeding lilac, which I loved
so fiercely.

Around me flat bodies of fishes.
And the enticing trickle of sand.

Oliver Behnssen

COEXISTENCE

An atoll crowded with doves,
laughing doves,
atom doves,
crowded with laughing atom doves,
atomic laughing doves,
doves of peace,
laughing doves of atom peace,
crowded with laughing doves of atomic peace,

ein Atoll voller Tauben
lacht,
ein Atoll lacht
lacht, lacht.

Ingeborg Bachmann

LIEDER AUF DER FLUCHT

I

Der Palmzweig bricht im Schnee,
die Stiegen stürzen ein,
die Stadt liegt steif und glänzt
im fremden Winterschein.

Die Kinder schreien und ziehn
den Hungerberg hinan,
sie essen vom weißen Mehl
und beten den Himmel an.

Der reiche Winterflitter,
das Mandarinengold,
treibt in den wilden Böen.
Die Blutorange rollt.

II

Ich aber liege allein
im Eisverhau voller Wunden.

Es hat mir der Schnee
noch nicht die Augen verbunden.

an atoll crowded with doves
laughs,
an atoll laughs,
laughs, laughs.

Ingeborg Bachmann

SONGS DURING FLIGHT

I

The snow-laden palm fronds break,
the stairs collapsed last night,
the town lies stiff and gleaming
in the strange wintry light.

The children scream and climb
the hunger mountain, up high,
they eat from the white flour
and worship the cold sky.

The lavish winter glitter,
the pale mandarin gold,
drift in wild gusts of wind.
Blood-red, the orange rolled.

II

But I am lying alone
in the barricade of ice

covered with wounds, and the snow
did not yet blindfold my eyes.

Die Toten, an mich gepreßt,
schweigen in allen Zungen.

Niemand liebt mich und hat
für mich eine Lampe geschwungen.

VI

Unterrichtet in der Liebe
durch zehntausend Bücher,
belehrt durch die Weitergabe
wenig veränderbarer Gesten
und törichter Schwüre—

eingeweiht in die Liebe
aber erst hier—
als die Lava herabfuhr
und ihr Hauch uns traf
am Fuß des Berges,
als zuletzt der erschöpfte Krater
den Schlüssel preisgab
für diese verschlossenen Körper—

Wir traten ein in verwunschene Räume
und leuchteten das Dunkel aus
mit den Fingerspitzen.

IX

Die schwarze Katze,
das Öl auf dem Boden,
der böse Blick:

Unglück!

Zieh das Korallenhorn
häng die Hörner vors Haus,
Dunkel, kein Licht!

Mute in foreign tongues
are corpses, pressed close to me.

No one loves me. No one swung
a lamp over me.

VI

Instructed about love
by ten thousand books,
taught love by the passing on
of almost unvarying gestures
and foolish vows—

but initiated into love
only here—
when the lava rode down
and its breath touched us
at the foot of the mountain,
until finally the exhausted crater
surrendered the key
to these sealed bodies—

We entered enchanted rooms
and explored the darkness
with the glowing tips of our fingers.

IX

The black cat,
oil on the floor,
the evil eye:

Disaster!

Blow the coral horn,
hang the goat's horn before the house.
Darkness, no light!

X

O Liebe, die unsre Schalen
aufbrach und fortwarf, unseren Schild,
den Wetterschutz und braunen Rost von Jahren!

O Leiden, die unsre Liebe austraten,
ihr feuchtes Feuer in den fühlenden Teilen!
Verqualmt, verendend im Qualm, geht die Flamme in sich.

XII

Mund, der in meinem Mund genächtigt hat,
Aug, das mein Aug bewachte,
Hand—

und die mich schleiften, die Augen!
Mund, der das Urteil sprach,
Hand, die mich hinrichtete!

XIII

Die Sonne wärmt nicht, stimmlos ist das Meer.
Die Gräber, schneeverpackt, schnürt niemand auf.
Wird denn kein Kohlenbecken angefüllt
mit fester Glut? Doch Glut tut's nicht.

Erlöse mich! Ich kann nicht länger sterben.

Der Heilige hat anderes zu tun;
er sorgt sich um die Stadt und geht ums Brot.
Die Wäscheleine trägt so schwer am Tuch;
bald wird es fallen. Doch mich deckt's nicht zu.

Ich bin noch schuldig. Heb mich auf.
Ich bin nicht schuldig. Heb mich auf.

X

O love, which broke and discarded
our shells, our shield,
protection from the weather and brown rust of years!

O suffering, which stamped out our love,
the smoldering fire in our feeling flesh!
Murky, dying in smoke, the flame sinks back into itself.

XII

Mouth, that rested in my mouth,
eyes, that watched over my eyes,
hand—

and how they dragged me through the dust! Those eyes.
Mouth, that passed judgment on me!
Hand, that put me to death.

XIII

The sun does not spend warmth, the sea is without voice,
graves, wrapped in snow. But no one unwraps them.
Is there no brazier filled with solid
embers? But embers will not help.

Deliver me! I can die no more.

The saint has other things to do,
he cares about the town and goes for bread.
The clothesline is overburdened with the sheet,
soon it will fall. It will not cover me.

I am still guilty. Lift me up.
I am not guilty. Lift me up.

Das Eiskorn lös vom zugefrornen Aug,
brich mit den Blicken ein,
die blauen Gründe such,
schwimm, schau und tauch:

Ich bin es nicht.
Ich bin's.

XV

Die Liebe hat einen Triumph und der Tod hat einen,
die Zeit und die Zeit danach.
Wir haben keinen.

Nur Sinken um uns von Gestirnen. Abglanz und Schweigen.
Doch das Lied überm Staub danach
wird uns übersteigen.

Ingeborg Bachmann

DIE GESTUNDETE ZEIT

Es kommen härtere Tage.
Die auf Widerruf gestundete Zeit
Wird sichtbar am Horizont.
Bald mußt du den Schuh schnüren
Und die Hunde zurückjagen in die Marschhöfe.

Denn die Eingeweide der Fische
Sind kalt geworden im Wind.
Ärmlich brennt das Licht der Lupinen.
Dein Blick spurt im Nebel:
Die auf Widerruf gestundete Zeit
Wird sichtbar am Horizont.

Melt from the frozen lids the grains of ice
and enter with your glance,
seek out the dark-blue bottom,
swim, look, and dive:

It is not I.
It is myself.

XV

Love has one triumph and death has one,
in this time and in the time thereafter.
We have none.

Only sinking of stars around us. Silence and afterglow.
But the song above the dust, thereafter,
will overtower us.

Ingeborg Bachmann

BORROWED TIME

Darker days are coming.
Time, our allotment withdrawn,
Becomes visible at the horizon.
Soon you must tie your shoes
And chase back the dogs to the farm in the marsh

For the entrails of the fish
Grow cold in the wind.
The light of the lupines burns poorly.
Your glance traces the fog:
Time, our allotment withdrawn,
Becomes visible at the horizon.

Drüben versinkt dir die Geliebte im Sand,
Er steigt um ihr wehendes Haar,
Er fällt ihr ins Wort,
Er befiehlt ihr zu schweigen,
Er findet sie sterblich
Und willig dem Abschied
Nach jeder Umarmung.

Sieh dich nicht um.
Schnür deinen Schuh.
Jag die Hunde zurück.
Wirf die Fische ins Meer.
Lösch die Lupinen!

Es kommen härtere Tage.

Günter Grass

DIE VORZÜGE DER WINDHÜHNER

Weil sie kaum Platz einnehmen
auf ihrer Stange aus Zugluft
und nicht nach meinen zahmen Stühlen picken.
Weil sie die harten Traumrinden nicht verschmähen,
nicht den Buchstaben nachlaufen,
die der Briefträger jeden Morgen vor meiner Tür verliert.
Weil sie stehen bleiben,
von der Brust bis zur Fahne
eine duldsame Fläche, ganz klein beschrieben,
keine Feder vergessen, kein Apostroph....
Weil sie die Tür offen lassen,
der Schlüssel die Allegorie bleibt,
die dann und wann kräht.

Beyond, your beloved sinks away from you into the sand,
It rises to her floating hair,
It smothers her speech,
It bids her to be silent,
It finds her mortal
And willing to part
After each embrace.

Do not look back.
Tie your shoes,
Chase back the dogs.
Throw the fish into the sea.
Quench the lupines!

Darker days are coming.

Günter Grass

THE MERITS OF THE WIND CHICKEN

Because they hardly take up any room
where they roost on their beam of air
and don't peck at my tame chairs.
Because they don't scorn the hard rind of dreams,
and don't run after the symbols
that the mailman loses at my door every morning.
Because they stand still,
from breast to tail-fan
one tolerant space, with tiny scribblings,
no feather forgotten, no apostrophe . . . .
Because they leave open the door,
and the key remains the allegory
crowing now and then.

Weil ihre Eier so leicht sind
und bekömmlich, durchsichtig.
Wer sah diesen Augenblick schon,
da das Gelb genug hat, die Ohren anlegt und verstummt.
Weil diese Stille so weich ist,
das Fleisch am Kinn einer Venus,
nähre ich sie.

Oft bei Ostwind,
wenn die Zwischenwände umblättern,
ein neues Kapitel sich auftut,
lehne ich glücklich am Zaun,
ohne die Hühner zählen zu müssen—
weil sie zahllos sind und sich ständig vermehren.

Günter Grass

GLEISDREIECK

Die Putzfraun ziehen von Ost nach West.
Nein Mann, bleib hier, was willst Du drüben;
komm rüber Mann, was willst du hier.

Gleisdreieck, wo mit heißer Drüse
die Spinne, die die Gleise legt,
sich Wohnung nahm und Gleise legt.

In Brücken geht sie nahtlos über
und schlägt sich selber Nieten nach,
wenn, was ins Netz geht, Nieten lockert.

Wir fahren oft und zeigen Freunden,
hier liegt Gleisdreieck, steigen aus
und zählen mit den Fingern Gleise.

Because their eggs are so light
and digestible, lucid.
Whoever saw the moment when
the yolk has enough, puts its ears back and is silent?
Because this silence is so soft,
flesh at the chin of a Venus,
that is why I feed them.

Often, in east wind,
when the partitions are turning over,
when a new chapter is opening up,
I lean full of happiness at the fence,
without having to count my chickens—
because they are countless and steadily increase.

Günter Grass

GLEISDREIECK*

The cleaning women move from East to West.
No, man, stay here, what do you want there?
Come over, man—what do you want here?

Gleisdreieck, that is where the spider
who spins the tracks is living now,
spinning tracks from its hot glands,

is clinching seamless tracks and bridges,
is tightening its own steel rivets
when what is caught loosens the rivets.

We often take the train and show
our friends Gleisdreieck. We get off
and count the tracks on our fingers.

Die Weichen locken, Putzfraun ziehn,
das Schlußlicht meint mich, doch die Spinne
fängt Fliegen und läßt Putzfraun ziehn.

Wir starren gläubig in die Drüse
und lesen, was die Drüse schreibt:
Gleisdreieck, Sie verlassen sogleich

Gleisdreieck und den Westsektor.

Günter Grass

BRANDMAUERN

Ich grüße Berlin, indem ich
dreimal meine Stirn an eine
der Brandmauern dreimal schlage.

Makellos ausgesägte,
wirft sie den Schatten dorthin,
wo früher dein Grundstück stand.

Persil und sein Blau überlebten
auf einer Mauer nach Norden;
nun schneit es, was gar nichts beweist.

Schwarz ohne Brandmauerinschrift
kommt mir die Mauer entgegen,
blickt sie mir über die Schulter.

Switches entice, charwomen move,
tail lights mean me, but the spider
catches the flies, lets charwomen move on.

We stare, faithful believers, at the gland
and read what the gland is writing:
"Gleisdreieck. You are about to leave

Gleisdreieck and the West Sector."

* Gleisdreieck, a station on the Berlin elevated railway in the middle of
Berlin, was a frontier crossing point between East and West before the
Wall was erected.

Günter Grass

BRANDMAUERN*

I greet Berlin as three times
I bang my head, three times
against one of the walls.

Faultlessly sawed out
it casts its shadow
where your house used to stand.

'Persil'** and its blue survived
on a blackened wall to the north;
now it is snowing—which proves nothing.

Black, without an inscription
the wall advances toward me,
looks over my shoulder.

Ein einziger Schneeball haftet.
Ein Junge warf ihn, weil etwas
tief in dem Jungen los war.

Günter Grass

IM EI

Wir leben im Ei.
Die Innenseite der Schale
haben wir mit unanständigen Zeichnungen
und den Vornamen unserer Feinde bekritzelt.
Wir werden gebrütet.

Wer uns auch brütet,
unseren Bleistift brütet er mit.
Ausgeschlüpft eines Tages,
werden wir uns sofort
ein Bildnis des Brütenden machen.

Wir nehmen an, daß wir gebrütet werden.
Wir stellen uns ein gutmütiges Geflügel vor
und schreiben Schulaufsätze
über Farbe und Rasse
der uns brütenden Henne.

Wann schlüpfen wir aus?
Unsere Propheten im Ei

One single snowball sticks.
A boy threw it because, deep down,
something is going on in the boy.

* *Brandmauer:* fireproof wall. The fireproof walls between houses were
usually the only ones left standing after heavy bombing, so the word
"Brandmauer" brings to the mind the burnt-out ruins of a city. Grass
also gives it the meaning here of the dividing lines between the East and
West zones in Berlin.

** *Persil:* a detergent.

Günter Grass

IN THE EGG

We are living in an egg.
On the inside of the shell
we scribbled indecent drawings
and the first names of our enemies.
We are being hatched.

Whosoever is hatching us
must hatch our pencils too.
After having crept out of the shell
we shall at once make
an image of our hatcher.

We assume we are being hatched.
We envisage a kind-hearted fowl
and write school papers
about the color and race
of the hen hatching us.

When shall we creep out?
For a mediocre salary

streiten sich für mittelmäßige Bezahlung
über die Dauer der Brutzeit.
Sie nehmen einen Tag X an.

Aus Langeweile und echtem Bedürfnis
haben wir Brutkästen erfunden.
Wir sorgen uns sehr um unseren Nachwuchs im Ei.
Gerne würden wir jener, die über uns wacht,
unser Patent empfehlen.

Wir aber haben ein Dach überm Kopf.
Senile Küken,
Embryos mit Sprachkenntnissen
reden den ganzen Tag
und besprechen noch ihre Träume.

Und wenn wir nun nicht gebrütet werden?
Wenn diese Schale niemals ein Loch bekommt?
Wenn unser Horizont nur der Horizont
unserer Kritzeleien ist und auch bleiben wird?
Wir hoffen, daß wir gebrütet werden.

Wenn wir auch nur noch vom Brüten reden,
bleibt doch zu befürchten, daß jemand,
außerhalb unserer Schale, Hunger verspürt,
uns in die Pfanne haut und mit Salz bestreut.
Was machen wir dann, ihr Brüder im Ei?

Horst Bienek

AVANT NOUS LE DÉLUGE

Sie wußten längst
Daß kein Platz mehr für sie
In der Arche war.

our prophets in the egg quarrel
about the length of hatching time.
They assume an X-Day.

Out of boredom and real need
we invented incubators.
We are much concerned about our progeny in the egg.
We would gladly recommend our patent
to the one who is watching over us.

We still have a roof over our heads.
Senile chicks,
embryos, versed in languages,
we talk all day long
and even discuss our dreams.

And what if we are not being hatched?
What if the shell should never break?
What if our horizon is only the horizon
of our scribbling, and will always remain so?
We still hope that we are being hatched.

Even though we talk of nothing but the hatching
we still fear that somebody
outside our shell may feel hungry,
break us into a pan and sprinkle salt on us.
What shall we do then, O brothers in the egg?

Horst Bienek

AVANT NOUS LE DÉLUGE

For a long time they knew
That there was no room
For them in the Ark.

Sie zogen traumentflammt
in die Ödnis der Berge
Und ließen sich dort
Als Fliehende registrieren.

Sie lehrten noch
Ihre Kinder das Beten,
Und daß es besser sei,
Auf dem Gipfel zu sterben,
Als unten im Dunkel.

Dann warteten sie
Auf das Steigen der Flut.
Sie wuschen zuerst darin
Ihre Füße in Demut
Und waren erschrocken,
Als sie erkannten,
Daß sie im Blut gebadet hatten.

Das machte ihr Sterben so furchtbar,
Daß sie im Blut ertrinken sollten.

Gerhard Neumann

FRÜHE

Taumorgen in
deinen Garten geschüttet.
Hebst du das bartrauhe Kinn.

Drängendes Schwellen:
Knospe will bersten
im Wechsel des Lichts.

Dream-fired, they withdrew
Into the bleak mountains
To be registered there
As fugitives.

They still taught
Their children how to pray,
And that it was better
To die upon a mountain
Than below, in darkness.

Then they waited
For the flood to rise.
At first they humbly washed
Their feet in it
And were alarmed
When they realized
That they had bathed in blood.

What made their dying horrible
Was that they drowned in blood.

Gerhard Neumann

DAWN

Dew-morning spilled
into your garden.
You lift a bristly chin.

Thrusting growth:
buds ready to burst
as the light changes.

Leicht wird die Zeit
unter steigenden Flügeln.
Brennt dir ein Wind auf der Haut.

Gerhard Neumann

DÄMMERUNG

Ich höre den Tritt auf den Treppen.
Tapeten wollen von den Wänden blättern.
Da ist die Tür aus gemasertem Holz,
mit der Farbe des Abends gestrichen:
du kommst.

Eine Haarkurve teilt dein Gesicht.
Wir wissen was ist, und was sein wird.
Laute flattern wie trunkne Insekten,
schaukeln auf den Wellen des Atems:
du sprichst.

Der Fußboden ist ein Schachbrett.
Zug um Zug nähern sich unsre Figuren.
Dann werden die Felder sich gleich.
Wir trinken aus einem einzigen Glas:
du bleibst.

Wolfgang Hädecke

DEUTSCHLAND

Dornen Zäune
die Töter dahinter
gelagert im Schnee

Time will be weightless
under rising wings.
Wind on your skin, burning.

Gerhard Neumann

DUSK

I hear steps on the stairs.
The wallpaper is ready to peel off.
There is the door of grained wood
painted in evening colors:
you are coming.

Curved hair parts your face.
We know what now is and what will be.
Sounds flutter like tipsy insects
swinging on the waves of your breath:
you are talking.

The floor is a chessboard.
Our figures draw nearer, move after move.
Then the chess-squares flow into one.
We are drinking from one single glass:
you remain.

Wolfgang Hädecke

GERMANY

Thorns fences
killers behind them
camped in snow

erbarme dich unser
im gelben Schnee
Wälder von Augen
Zäune im Dorn
niemand erbarmt sich
der Augen im Dorn

Schnee eines weißen Herzens
dahinter Wälder von Tötern
mit gelben Augen
Zäune im Herzen aus Schnee
erbarme dich nicht
Dorn meines Herzens
Töter am Dornenzaun
gelbe Wälder voll Schnee
niemand weiß es
niemand erbarmt sich

über dem gelben Wald
die Augen der Töter
gelagert im weißen Herzen
über dem gelben Dorn
teilt die Leuchtspur
den Schnee.

Wolfgang Hädecke

TELTOWKANAL

Zwischen Weide und Damm
der Fisch, im Ölwasser, Menschenfisch,
silbern die Nackenflosse, das Haar
im öligen Schaum, ein stummer
tauchender grauer Menschenfisch,

have mercy upon us
in yellow snow
woods of eyes
fences of thorns
nobody has mercy
on the eyes in the thorn

Snow of white heart
and woods with killers
with yellow eyes
fences in snow-hearts
have no mercy
thorn of my heart
killers at thorny fences
yellow woods under snow
nobody knows
nobody has mercy

over yellow woods
eyes of killers
camped in white hearts
over yellow thorn
a flaring trace is parting
the snow.

Wolfgang Hädecke

TELTOW CANAL IN BERLIN

Between willows and levee
a fish in the oily water, human fish,
silvery the back-fin, his hair
in oily foam, a silent gray
human fish, diving,

dicht bei den Reusen, im Nachtwasser,
keuchend, das Nackensegel gesetzt:

Schüsse. Schüsse. Schüsse:
die Blutperlenspur im Öl, in der Nacht,
und der Weidentod greift mit dem Lichtarm,
dem Arm des Kraken das silberne Segel,
er wirft den Fisch in die Luft,
in die Nachtluft, den Menschenfisch, grau,
die Bauchflosse leuchtet:

„Und wär's nur um diesen, den einen,
ich sage euch, dieser, der eine,
versinkend im Schlamm, er ist es . . . ."

Vier Uhr. Vier Uhr.
Und das Öl. Und die Winde. Die Nacht.

Wolfgang Hädecke

VORM EINSCHLAFEN ZU SPRECHEN

Gib deinen Mund—wir fallen schwer und langsam
ins feiste Kraut, ins Nest der blauen Käfer
wir haben Farn und Wurzel an den Hüften
und einen Mond im Auge: blaß und rund.

Nimm mich beim Hals—mir klopfen alle Adern
mir schwemmt die Müdigkeit das Blut vom Herzen
ich wärme Worte, atme Nacht und sinke
an dir vorbei und mondwärts auf den Schlaf.

Bleibst du noch wach? —wir schwimmen durch die Wasser
des Traumes zwischen Tang und Fels und Fisch:
ich—schweres Boot und Algen an den Planken,
du—Segel, weiß und leicht im großen Wind.

near the wicker-traps, in night-darkened water,
panting, his back-sail set:

Shots. Shots. Shots:
a string of bloodied pearls in the oil, in the night.
Willow-death, with arms of light, arms of an octopus,
is reaching for the silvery sail,
he throws the fish into the air,
night air, the human fish, gray,
belly fins are gleaming:

"And if it were only for this one, for this one,
I tell you, this one, the one,
sinking in foam, he is it...."

Four A. M. Four A. M.
And the oil. The wind. The night.

Wolfgang Hädecke

SONG BEFORE FALLING ASLEEP

Give me your lips—heavily, slowly, we sink
into the weeds, into the nests of bluish beetles,
fern and roots we feel at our hips,
a moon in our eyes: pale and round.

Put your arms around my neck—my veins are pounding,
tiredness washes the blood away now from my heart,
I warm my words, I breathe the night, and sink
away from you, toward the moon, and toward sleep.

Are you awake still? —we are drifting through the flood
of dreams, through seaweed, rocks and fish:
I—heavy boat, barnacles at the planks,
you—sail, so white and light in the great wind.

Thomas Bernhard

Das Jahr ist wie das Jahr vor tausend Jahren,
wir tragen den Krug und schlagen den Rücken der Kuh,
wir mähen und wissen nichts vom Winter,
wir trinken Most und wissen nichts,
bald werden wir vergessen sein
und die Verse zerfallen wie Schnee vor dem Haus.

Das Jahr ist wie das Jahr vor tausend Jahren,
wir schauen in den Wald wie in den Stall der Welt,
wir lügen und flechten Körbe für Äpfel und Birnen,
wir schlafen während unsre beschmutzten Schuhe
vor der Haustür verwittern.

Das Jahr ist wie das Jahr vor tausend Jahren,
wir wissen nichts,
wir wissen nichts vom Untergang,
von den versunkenen Städten, vom Strom in dem Pferde
und Menschen ertrunken sind.

Thomas Bernhard

Meine Verzweiflung kommt um Mitternacht
und schaut mich an als wär ich lange tot
die Augen schwarz und müd die Stirn vor Blüten,
der bittere Honig meiner Traurigkeit
tropft auf die kranke Erde nieder
die mich in roten Nächten wachhält oft
zu sehn des Herbstes unruhvolles Sterben.

Thomas Bernhard

THE YEAR IS LIKE
THE YEAR A THOUSAND YEARS AGO

The year is like the year a thousand years ago;
we carry the jug and whip the back of the cow,
we mow the grass and know nothing of winter,
we drink new wine and know nothing,
soon we shall be forgotten
and our songs will fade like snow at the doorsill.

The year is like the year a thousand years ago;
we gaze into the wood as if into the stable of the world,
we deceive and we weave baskets for apples and for pears,
we sleep while our dirtied shoes
lie crumbling at the doorsill.

The year is like the year a thousand years ago;
we know nothing,
we know nothing of doom,
of lost cities, of the river where horses
and people drowned.

Thomas Bernhard

MY DESPERATION BEGINS AT MIDNIGHT

My desperation begins at midnight,
staring at me as if I had died long ago,
eyes black, the forehead tired of blossoms,
the bitter honey of my sorrow
dripping upon the sickly earth,
often keeping me awake in red nights
to watch the autumn's restless dying.

Meine Verzweiflung kommt um Mitternacht
aus den verworrenen Träumen der Sonne und des Regens,
früh sag ich, daß ich alles lobte
und fremd bin meiner Tür und meiner Angst,
vieltausend Jahre stürzen aus den kalten Wänden
und tragen mich ein Stück dem Winter zu.

Meine Verzweiflung kommt um Mitternacht
verändert ist das Tal, der Mond schwimmt auf den Wiesen,
des zornigen Abends zerbrochene Sichel lehnt
am Fensterbrett und schaut mich an.
Ich weiß genau, daß ich zerschlagen bin
wie diese Sichel, keiner täuscht mich jetzt,
auch nicht der Fluß der seinen Spruch
noch vor dem Morgen fällt.

Thomas Bernhard

Im Garten der Mutter
sammelt mein Rechen die Sterne,
die herabgefallen sind, während ich fort war.
Die Nacht ist warm, und meine Glieder
strömen die grüne Herkunft aus,
Blumen und Blätter,
den Amselruf und das Klatschen des Webstuhls.
Im Garten der Mutter
trete ich barfuß auf die Schlangenköpfe,
die durch das rostige Tor hereinschaun
mit feurigen Zungen.

My desperation begins at midnight
from mottled dreams of sun and rain.
At dawn I say that I praise all that is.
I am a stranger to my door and to my fear.
Thousands of years are tumbling from cold walls
and carry me along toward winter.

My desperation begins at midnight.
The valley is changed, the moon swims in the meadows
The angry evening's broken sickle leans
against the windowsill and looks at me.
I know it now that I am broken
like this sickle. No one deceives me now,
not even the river passing sentence
before the day breaks.

Thomas Bernhard

IN MY MOTHER'S GARDEN

In my mother's garden
my rake gathers the stars
that fell down while I was away.
The night is warm, and my limbs
radiate their green origin,
flowers and leaves,
song of the thrush and click of the loom.
In my mother's garden
I step barefooted on the heads of snakes
that stare at me through the rusty gate
with fiery tongues.

Christoph Meckel

BALLADE

Ich rufe eine schwarze Sonne, schrie
der Hahn im weißen Dampf auf schwarzem Mist.
Geschrei verscheuchte Schlummer aller Höfe.

Die Schwalben stoben in den kalten Regen
der Maulwurf tappte blind durch nasse Blumen
und Ochsen stampften brummend aus den Ställen.

Und Mägde rannten barfuß in die Wälder
und Knechte eilten fort auf alten Gäulen—
der Bauer weinte wild: Ach Hahn, mein Hähnchen!

Da hinter siebenfachem Regen stieg
die Sonne schwarz und schnell, stand ohne Laut,
und krachte finster auf die Ebnen nieder.

Christoph Meckel

DIE BEUTE

Bringt sie mir, tot
oder lebend, befahl ich,
und meine Jäger, heimkehrend
von langen Jagden aus allen Wäldern
reichten mir die tote Beute durchs Fenster ins Haus
bis sich mein Haus
mit Leibern unendlich füllte.

Christoph Meckel

BALLAD

I'm calling a black sun! The rooster crowed
on his dungheap through white mists.
Wild screams killed sleep in every homestead.

Swallows scattered in the chilling rain,
a mole groped blindly through wet flowers
and oxen plodded grumbling from the stable.

The servant girls ran barefoot to the woods,
the farmhands rushed away on toddering nags—
wildly the peasant wept: O rooster! little rooster!

Then from behind the sevenfold dark rain
the sun rose, black and swift, stood still without a sound,
and then crashed, darkening, down upon the land.

Christoph Meckel

THE PREY

Bring them to me, dead
or alive, I commanded,
and my hunters homecoming
from long chases in the woods
heaved the kill through the windows
until my house was filled
with carcasses, infinitely.

Fliegende Fische, Engel,
und Riesen in Königsgewändern
habe ich, Tote alle, beherbergt in meinen Wänden
versucht in ihren leeren Augen zu lesen
betastet, geküßt ihre Münder
belauert belacht
geheult um ein Zeichen, geschrien—und bald
die Beute in die Wälder zurückbringen heißen.

Christoph Meckel

GOLDFISCH

Seit ich den Mond und das Wasser liebe,
Lebt ein Goldfisch in meinem Haar,
Das verblüfft mich und ich bemerke,
Daß das bei keinem anderen Menschen der Fall ist.

Seither bin ich durch viele Flüsse geschwommen,
Aber das Wasser sagte ihm nicht zu.
Ich bot ihn dem Mann im Mond als Geschenk,
Doch er weigerte sich, im Licht der Sterne

Zwischen den Wolken und Vögeln zu schwimmen;
Ich führte ihn an das Rote Meer,
Aber er besteht darauf
In der Dämmerung meines Herzens zu altern.

Ich werde ihn weitertragen,
Bis seine Schuppen bröckeln,
Bis er schwarz wird
Und tot in eine graue Pfütze fällt.

Flying fish, angels,
giants in kingly raiment—
I sheltered them, dead all of them,
inside my four walls.
I tried to read in their glazed eyes,
I touched them, kissed their mouths,
spied, laughed at them,
howled for a sign, screamed—
and soon I bade my hunters
to take back the prey, back to the woods.

Christoph Meckel

THE GOLDFISH

Because I love the moon and the water
A goldfish has been living in my hair.
This puzzles me since I notice
That this is not the case with other people.

I have swum in many rivers
But water does not agree with my goldfish.
I offered it as a gift to the man in the moon
But it refused to swim in the light of the stars

Among clouds and birds;
I took it to the Red Sea
But it insists
On growing old in the dusk of my heart.

I have to go on wearing it
Until its scales crumble,
Until it turns black
And falls, dead, into a gray puddle.

hans magnus enzensberger

verteidigung der wölfe gegen die lämmer

soll der geier vergißmeinnicht fressen?
was verlangt ihr vom Schakal,
daß er sich häute, vom wolf? soll
er sich selber ziehen die zähne?
was gefällt euch nicht
an politruks und an päpsten,
was guckt ihr blöd aus der wäsche
auf den verlogenen bildschirm?

wer näht denn dem general
den blutstreif an seine hose? wer
zerlegt vor dem wucherer den kapaun?
wer hängt sich stolz das blechkreuz
vor den knurrenden nabel? wer
nimmt das trinkgeld, den silberling,
den schweigepfennig? es gibt
viel bestohlene, wenig diebe; wer
applaudiert ihnen denn, wer
steckt die abzeichen an, wer
lechzt nach der lüge?

seht in den spiegel: feig,
scheuend die mühsal der wahrheit,
dem lernen abgeneigt, das denken
überantwortend den wölfen,
der nasenring euer teuerster schmuck,
keine täuschung zu dumm, kein trost
zu billig, jede erpressung
ist für euch noch zu milde.

hans magnus enzensberger

whitewashing wolves

should vultures feed on forget-me-nots?
what do you expect of jackals,
must the wolf skin himself?
must he pull his own teeth?
what do you dislike
in commissars and popes?
why do you gape from your stiff collars
at the deceitful screen?

who sews the blood-red stripes
on the general's pants?
who carves the capon for the usurer?
who proudly hangs the tinny medal
in front of his rumbling navel?
who takes the tip, the shekel,
the hush money?
many are robbed, thieves are only a few;
who, then, applauds them,
who wears the badge,
who craves the lie?

look in the mirror: cringing,
shrinking from the hardship of truth,
unwilling to learn, abandoning
thought to the wolves,
a ring through the nose your most
precious possession,
no deception too stupid, no consolation
too cheap, every blackmail
is still too mild for you.

ihr lämmer, schwestern sind,
mit euch verglichen, die krähen:
ihr blendet einer den andern.
brüderlichkeit herrscht
unter den wölfen:
sie gehn in rudeln.

gelobt sein die räuber: ihr,
einladend zur vergewaltigung,
werft euch aufs faule bett
des gehorsams, winselnd noch
lügt ihr. zerrissen
wollt ihr werden. ihr
ändert die welt nicht.

hans magnus enzensberger

anweisung an sisyphos

was du tust, ist aussichtslos. gut:
du hast es begriffen, gib es zu,
aber finde dich nicht damit ab,
mann mit dem stein. niemand
dankt dir; kreidestriche,
der regen leckt sie gelangweilt auf,
markieren den tod, freu dich nicht
zu früh, das aussichtslose
ist keine karriere. mit eigener
tragik duzen sich wechselbälge,
vogelscheuchen, auguren. schweig,
sprich mit der sonne ein wort,
während der stein rollt, aber
labe dich an deiner ohnmacht nicht,

you lambs, compared with you
crows are sisters;
you peck at each others' eyes.
fraternity rules
among wolves:
they travel in packs.

praised be the robbers:
you, inviting rape,
throw yourself down on the slovenly bed
of obedience, whining,
and still you are lying.
you want to be torn to pieces.
you won't change the world.

hans magnus enzensberger

instructions for sisyphus

what you are doing is hopeless. all right:
you understand that; admit it
but do not be contented with it,
man with the rock. no one is going
to thank you; chalk-lines,
that a dull rain is licking away,
are marking death. do not rejoice
too early; hopelessness
is no career. only changelings,
scarecrows, augurs are on easy terms
with their own tragedy. be silent,
say a word to the sun,
while the rock is rolling, but
do not relish your impotence,

sondern vermehre um einen zentner
den zorn der welt, um ein gran.
es herrscht ein mangel an männern,
das aussichtslose stumm tuend,
ausraufend wie gras die hoffnung,
ihr gelächter, die zukunft, rollend,
rollend ihren zorn auf die berge.

hans magnus enzensberger

konjunktur

ihr glaubt zu essen
aber das ist kein fleisch
womit sie euch füttern
das ist köder, das schmeckt süß
(vielleicht vergessen die angler
die schnur, vielleicht
haben sie ein gelübde getan,
in zukunft zu fasten?)

der haken schmeckt nicht nach biscuit
er schmeckt nach blut
er reißt euch aus der lauen brühe:
wie kalt ist die luft an der beresina!
ihr werdet euch wälzen
auf einem fremden sand
einem fremden eis:
grönland, nevada, fest-
krallen sich eure glieder
im fell der nubischen wüste.

sorgt euch nicht! gutes gedächtnis
ziert die angler, alte erfahrung.

but increase the wrath of the world
by a hundredweight, by a grain.
there is a lack of men
silently doing what is hopeless,
weeding out hope, rolling
their laughter, the future,
rolling their wrath uphill on the mountains.

hans magnus enzensberger

boom

you think you are eating
but it is not meat
that they feed you—
it is bait, it tastes sweet
(maybe the fishermen will forget
the line, maybe
they've made a vow
to fast in future?)

the hook does not taste like biscuit
it tastes like blood
as it hauls you out of the tepid broth:
how cold the air is on the beresina!
you will wallow
on foreign sand
on foreign ice:
greenland, nevada, your limbs
will clutch the hide
of the nubian desert.

don't worry! a good memory
serves the fishermen, an old knowledge.

sie tragen zu euch die liebe
des metzgers zu seiner sau.
sie sitzen geduldig am rhein,
am potomac, an der beresina,
an den flüssen der welt.
sie weiden euch. sie warten.

ihr schlagt euch das gebiß in die hälse.
euch vor dem hunger fürchtend
kämpft ihr um den tödlichen köder.

hans magnus enzensberger

auf das grab eines friedlichen mannes

dieser da war kein menschenfreund,
mied versammlungen, kaufhäuser, arenen;
seinesgleichen fleisch aß er nicht.

auf den straßen ging die gewalt
lächelnd, nicht nackt;
aber es waren schreie am himmel.

die gesichter der leute waren nicht deutlich;
sie schienen zertrümmert,
noch ehe der schlag gefallen war.

eines, um das er zeitlebens gekämpft hat,
mit wörtern und zähnen, ingrimmig,
hinterlistig, auf eigene faust:

das ding, das er seine ruhe nannte,
da er es hat, nun ist kein mund mehr
an seinem gebein, es zu schmecken.

they love you with the love
a butcher has for his sow.
patiently they sit on the rhine,
on the potomac, on the beresina,
on the rivers of the world.
they lead you to pasture. they wait.

you sink your fangs into each others' throats.
afraid of hunger,
you fight for the deadly bait.

hans magnus enzensberger

to the grave of a peace-loving man

this one was no philanthropist,
avoided meetings, department stores, arenas;
he never ate the flesh of his like.

violence walked in the streets,
smiling, not naked;
but there were screams in the sky.

people's faces were indistinct;
they seemed crushed
even before the blow fell.

the one thing he had fought for all his life
with words and with teeth, grimly,
cunningly, on his own account:

the thing he called his peace,
now, that he has it: there is no mouth
to his skeleton now, no mouth to taste it.

hans magnus enzensberger

call it love

jetzt summen in den nackten häusern die körbe
auf und nieder
                lodern die lampen
                        betäubend
schlägt der april durchs gläserne laub
springen den frauen die pelze im park auf
ja über den dächern
                  preisen die diebe
                        den abend
als hätte wie eine taube aus weißem batist
als hätte unvermutet und weiß und schimmernd
die verschollene hinter den bergen, den formeln,
die ausgewiesene auf den verwitterten sternen,
ohne gedächtnis
                verbannt
                  ohne paß ohne schuhe
sich niedergelassen auf ihre bittern
todmüden jäger
                schön ist der abend

hans magnus enzensberger

lock lied

meine weisheit ist eine binse
schneide dich in den finger damit
um ein rotes ideogramm zu pinseln
auf meine schulter
ki wit   ki wit

hans magnus enzensberger

call it love

now the baskets hum up and down
in the naked houses
                          lamps flare
                                    april
crashes shockingly through glassy leaves
the ladies' fur coats fly open in the park
across the roofs
                    the thieves praise
                                  the evening
as if—like a dove of white gauze—
as if—unexpected and white and shimmering—
the utterly lost, beyond the mountains, beyond the forms,
the exiled upon the crumbling stars,
banished
                without memory
                                without passport   without shoes
descended upon its bitter
deadly tired hunters
                          the evening is beautiful

hans magnus enzensberger

bird lure

my wisdom is a reed
cut your finger with it
and draw a red ideogram
on my shoulder
kee wit   kee wit

meine schulter ist ein schnelles schiff
leg dich auf das sonnige deck
um zu einer insel zu schaukeln
aus glas   aus rauch
ki wit

meine stimme ist ein sanftes verlies
laß dich nicht fangen
meine binse ist ein seidener dolch
hör nicht zu
ki wit   ki wit   ki wit

hans magnus enzensberger

schläferung

laß mich heut nacht in der gitarre schlafen
in der verwunderten gitarre der nacht
laß mich ruhn
          im zerbrochenen holz
laß meine hände schlafen
               auf ihren saiten
meine verwunderten hände
            laß schlafen
das süße holz
       laß meine saiten
            laß die nacht
auf den vergessenen griffen ruhn
meine zerbrochenen hände
            laß schlafen
auf den süßen saiten
im verwunderten holz

my shoulder is a speedy ship
lie down on the sunny deck
and rock to an island
of glass   of smoke
kee wit

my voice is a gentle snare
do not get caught
my reed is a silken dagger
do not listen
kee wit   kee wit   kee wit

hans magnus enzensberger

lulling to sleep

let me sleep tonight in the guitar
in the bewildered guitar of night
let me rest
                in the broken wood
let my hands sleep
                        upon its strings
let my startled hands
                        sleep
in the sweet wood
                let my strings
                        let the night
rest upon the forgotten chords
let my broken hands
                        rest
upon the sweet strings
in the bewildered wood

hans magnus enzensberger

landnahme

das ich gegründet habe mit meinen augen,
das ich mit meinen heutigen händen halte,
mein land, mein sterbliches land,
leuchtend von meiner freude,
die hat dich zu mir verwünscht
für die fremde und die vertraute zeit,
für alle zeiten, die uns geblieben sind.

ich sage dir deinen namen, sprich
und gib mir die sprache wieder
aus deinem sprachlosen mund.

mein land, ich verschone dich nicht,
ich halte dich, selber sterblich,
in dieses sterbliche licht.

wir sind nah, widerstrahlend
einer von dem schönen sommer des andern,
mein land, wie der schatten des ölbaums leicht
benetze ich deine warme grenze,
die atmet in ihrem glanz,
und wie des ölbaums schatten, ausdauernd
gegen das verderben will ich auf dir ruhn,

mein unermeßliches land,
das ich umspannen kann mit meinen ellen,
mein vertrauter weltteil, so groß
wie eines ölbaums schatten, wie ein grab,
blühend gegen den blutigen schutt
der zeiten, die uns geblieben sind.

hans magnus enzensberger

taking of the land

which i founded with my eyes,
which i hold with today's hands,
my land, my mortal land,
glowing with my joy
which bewitched me for you
in strange and in familiar times,
in all the times remaining for us.

i shall tell you your name, speak
and give me back my speech
from your speechless mouth.

my land, i do not spare you,
i hold you, mortal myself,
into this mortal light.

we are close, radiant
one with the fair summer of the other,
my land, light like an olive tree's shadow
i shall bless your warm boundary
breathing in its glow,
and like an olive tree's shadow
persevering against ruin
i shall rest upon you,

my infinite land,
which i can enfold in my arms,
my familiar part of the globe, as large
as an olive tree's shadow, as a grave,
flowering against the gory rubble
of the times remaining for us.

NOTES ON THE POETS

The bibliographical listings are selective: the most important German volumes of each poet and translated U.S. editions where available. Publishers will be found in the acknowledgments on page XI.

P: Poetry; N: Novel; Sst: Short story; RP: Radio play; Ant: Anthology; Ess: Essay.

ARP, Hans (Jean). Born 1887 Strasbourg, Alsace. Co-founder of Dadaism, 1916. Has been living in Meudon near Paris since 1926. Influential abstract sculptor, painter, lyricist in German and French. Surrealistic and Dadaistic poetry. Collected German work published by Limes Verlag. On *My Way* (poetry and essays), Wittenborn, N.Y., 1948.

BACHMANN, Ingeborg. Born 1926 Klagenfurt, Austria. Studied in Vienna, is now living in Berlin. Lyrics, short stories, radio plays. *Die gestundete Zeit*, P, 1953; *Anrufung des großen Bären*, P, 1956; *Der gute Gott von Manhattan*, RP, 1958; *Das dreißigste Jahr*, Sst, 1961; *Prinz von Homburg*, libretto for an opera by Hans Werner Henze, 1962. *The Thirtieth Year*, Sst, Knopf, N.Y., 1964.

BEHNSSEN, Oliver. Born 1925 Breslau. Lives in Munich. Poems in magazines and anthologies.

BENDER, Hans. Born 1919 Mühlhausen. Prisoner of war in Russia till 1949. Lives in Cologne. Editor of *Junge Lyrik*, yearly anthology; coeditor of literary magazine, *Akzente*. Lyricist, novelist. *Fremde soll vorüber sein*, P, 1951; *Eine Sache wie die Liebe*, N, 1954; *Wunschkost*, N, 1959; *Mit dem Postschiff*, Sst, 1962.

BENN, Gottfried. M.D. and poet. Born 1886 in the Mark Brandenburg, son and grandson of ministers; his mother was a French-Swiss. He died in Berlin in 1956. One of the most influential writers of his time in Germany. Besides poetry he wrote essays, short stories, plays—37 books in all. *Gesammelte Werke*, IV vols., 1959-61. *Primal Vision* (selected writings), N.Y., New Directions, 1960.

BERNHARD, Thomas. Born 1931 in Holland, of Austrian descent. Studied music and drama in Vienna. Lives mostly in Carinthia. Poetry, short stories, novel. *Auf der Erde und in der Hölle*, P, 1957; *Unter dem Eisen des Mondes*, P, 1958; *Frost*, N, 1963.

BIENEK, Horst. Born 1930 in Silesia. Studied under Brecht in Berlin, was deported to Siberia in 1951, returned in 1955. Lives in Frankfurt am Main. Publisher's reader. *Traumbuch eines Gefangenen*, P, 1957; *Werkstattgespräche*, Ess, 1962.

BOBROWSKI, Johannes. Born 1917 Tilsit, East Prussia. Lives in East Berlin. Publisher's reader. *Sarmatische Zeit*, P, 1961; *Schattenland Ströme*, P, 1962.

BRAMBACH, Rainer. Born 1917 Basel, Switzerland. Was a farm hand, peatcutter, gardener. Lives in Switzerland. Lyricist. *Tagwerk*, P, 1959; *Wahrnehmungen*, sketches, 1961.

BRECHT, Bertolt. Born 1898 Augsburg, died 1956 in Berlin. Son of well-to-do parents. Was a radical nihilist, later on a Marxist. Left Germany as early as February, 1933; his books were officially burned in May, 1933. Lived in Switzerland, France, Denmark, Finland. Fled 1941 via Vladivostok to California, where he lived for six years. Subpoenaed by House Un-American Activities Committee, Washington, 1947. Left for Switzerland, the only country that would admit him; waited for half a year for permission from the Allied Military Government to return to West Germany. In 1948, went to East Berlin with a Czechoslovakian passport. Founded the Berliner Ensemble in 1949, stage director of the Deutsche Theatre. Collected work is being published by Suhrkamp Verlag, Frankfurt am Main and Aufbau Verlag, East Berlin. *Stücke*, XII vols., 1953-'59; *Versuche*, XV vols., 1930-'57; *Gedichte*, VII, 1961, ff.; *Schriften zum Theatre*, VI, 1963, ff. *Threepenny Novel*, N.Y., Grove, 1956; *Parables for the Theater*, N.Y., Grove, 1957; *Selected Poems*, N.Y., Grove, 1959; *Kalendergeschichten*, N.Y., Norton, 1960; *Selected Plays*, N.Y., Grove, 1961.

BUSTA, Christine. Born 1915 Vienna, where she now lives. Librarian. Lyricist. *Lampe und Delphin*, P, 1955; *Die Scheune der Vögel*, P, 1958; *Die Sternenmühle*, P, 1959.

CELAN, Paul. Born 1920 Chernovtsy, Rumania. Studied medicine in Bucharest, fled to Vienna in 1947, to Paris in 1948, where he has been living since. Translations from Russian and French. *Der Sand aus den Urnen*, P, 1948; *Mohn und Gedächtnis*, P, 1952; *Von Schwelle zu Schwelle*, P, 1955; *Sprachgitter*, P, 1959; *Die Niemandsrose*, P, 1963.

DOMIN, Hilde. Born 1912 Cologne. Studied in Germany and Italy. Teacher in England, Latin America. Returned to Germany in 1954. Translations from Spanish. *Nur eine Rose als Stütze*, P, 1959; *Rückkehr der Schiffe*, P, 1961.

EICH, Günter. Born 1907 Silesia. Studied Sinology and law. Lives in Bavaria. Gave great impetus to German radio play writing. *Abgelegene Gehöfte*,

P, 1948; *Untergrundbahn*, P, 1949; *Botschaften des Regens*, P, 1955; *Allah hat hundert Namen*, RP, 1958; *Stimmen*, RP's, 1960; *Ausgewählte Gedichte*, P, 1960.

ENZENSBERGER, hans magnus. Born 1929 in Bavaria. Drafted into the army at age 16. Later tramped through Europe and U.S.A., studied in Germany and France. Lives in Norway. Translations from English, French, Spanish, Norwegian, Dutch. Monthly column in *Der Spiegel*. Lyricist and essayist. *verteidigung der wölfe*, P, 1957; *landessprache*, P, 1960; *museum der modernen poesie*, anthology in 14 languages, 1960; *Gedichte*, P, 1962; *Einzelheiten*, Ess, 1962.

GONG, Alfred. Born 1920 Chernovtsy, Rumania. Studied in Vienna. Has been living in New York since 1951. *Gras und Omega*, P, 1960; *Manifest Alpha*, P, 1961; *Interview mit Amerika*, Ant., 1962.

GRASS, Günter. Born 1927 Danzig. Novelist, playwright, graphic artist, sculptor. Lives in West Berlin. *Vorzüge der Windhühner*, P, 1956; *Die Blechtrommel*, N, 1959; *Gleisdreieck*, P, 1960; *Katz und Maus*, N, 1961; *Hundejahre*, N, 1963. *The Tin Drum*, Pantheon, N.Y., 1963; *Cat and Mouse*, Harcourt, N.Y., 1963.

HÄDECKE, Wolfgang. Born 1929 Weissenfels/Saale, East Germany. A book of poetry, *Uns stehen die Fragen auf*, published in 1958, led to political attacks. Left for West Germany in 1958. Lives in Bielefeld. *Leuchtspur im Schnee*, P, 1963.

HAGELSTANGE, Rudolf. Born 1912 Nordhausen (Harz). Lives in Unteruhldingen/Bodensee. Lyricist and novelist. *Venetianisches Credo*, P, 1945; *Strom der Zeit*, P, 1948; *Ballade vom verschütteten Leben*, P, 1952; *Zwischen Stern und Staub*, P, 1953; *How Do You Like America?*, Ess, 1957; *Spielball der Götter*, N, 1959; *Lied der Jahre*, P, 1961; *Die Puppen in der Puppe*, Ess, 1963; *Ballad of the Buried Life*, U. of N.C. Press, 1962.

HEISSENBÜTTEL, Helmut. Born 1921 Wilhelmshaven. Lives in Stuttgart. *Kombinationen*, P, 1954; *Textbuch 1, 2, 3*, P, 1960/61/62.

HILTY, Hans Rudolf. Born 1925 St. Gallen, Switzerland, where he still lives. Founder and editor of the poetry magazine *Hortulus*. *Eingebrannt in den Schnee*, P, 1956; *Parsival*, N, 1962.

HÖLLERER, Walter. Born 1922 Bavaria. Professor and critic in Berlin. Co-editor of literary magazine, *Akzente*. *Der andere Gast*, P, 1952; *Transit* (Ant. of modern German poetry), 1956.

HOLTHUSEN, Hans Egon. Born 1913 Rendsburg. Since 1961 program director of Goethe House, N.Y. Poet and literary critic. *Labyrinthische Jahre*, P, 1952; *Ja und Nein*, Ess, 1954; *Das Schiff*, N, 1956; *Das Schöne und das*

Wahre, Ess, 1958; *Kritisches Verstehen*, Ess, 1961; *Unbewältigte Vergangenheit*, Ess, 1963; *R. M. Rilke*, New Haven, Yale U. P. 1952; *The Crossing*, N, London, Deutsch, 1959.

HUCHEL, Peter. Born 1903 Berlin, lives in Wilhelmshorst near Potsdam. From 1948 till 1962 he was editor of the East German literary magazine *Sinn und Form*. *Gedichte*, P, 1948; *Chausseen Chausseen*, P, 1963.

JOKOSTRA, Peter. Born 1912 Dresden. Teacher and critic in Chemnitz, fled to the West in 1958, lives in Linz on the Rhine. *An der besonnten Mauer*, P, 1958; *Magische Strasse*, P, 1960; *Hinab zu den Sternen*, P, 1961; *Herzinfarkt*, N, 1961; *Die Zeit hat keine Ufer*, Diary, 1963.

JÜNGER, Friedrich Georg. Born 1898 Hannover, lives in Überlingen on Lake Constance. Has 32 books to his credit, 11 of them poetry. Also novels, essays, short stories. *Der Taurus*, P, 1937; *Die Perfection der Technik*, Ess, 1946; *Die Perlenschnur*, P, 1947, *Iris im Wind*, P, 1952; *Schwarzer Fluß und windweißer Wald*, P, 1955; *Zwei Schwestern*, N, 1956; *Sprache und Denken*, Ess, 1962; *Failure of Technology*, Regnery, Chicago, 1949.

KASCHNITZ, Marie Luise. Born 1901 in Karlsruhe, lives in Frankfurt am Main and Rome. Poetry and Prose. Has published 18 books. *Gedichte*, P, 1947; *Zukunftsmusik*, P, 1950; *Das dicke Kind*, N, 1952; *Ewige Stadt*, P, 1952; *Das Haus der Kindheit*, Autobiog., 1956; *Lange Schatten*, Sst, 1960; *Dein Schweigen meine Stimme*, P, 1962; *Wohin denn ich*, Ess, 1963.

KROLOW, Karl. Born 1915 Hanover, lives in Darmstadt. Poetry and translations from Spanish and French. 10 books of poetry. *Hochgelobtes gutes Leben*, P, 1943; *Heimsuchung*, P, 1948; *Wind und Zeit*, P, 1954; *Anthology of French Poetry*, 1957; *Fremde Körper*, P, 1959; *Unsichtbare Hände*, P, 1962.

LAVANT, Christine. Born 1915 St. Stefan, Austria, where she lives. Partially blind and deaf. *Die Bettlerschale*, P, 1956; *Spindel im Mond*, P, 1959; *Der Pfauenschrei*, P, 1962.

LEHMANN, Wilhelm. Born 1882 in Venezuela of German parents, grew up in Germany, lives in Eckernförde, Holstein. Novels, essays, 8 books of poetry. Lyricist of great influence. *Sämtliche Werke*, III vols. 1962.

LEIP, Hans. Born 1893 Hamburg, lives at Fruthwilen, Thurgau, Switzerland. Novels, plays, verse. (Author of "Lily Marleen.") Has 34 books published. *Der Nigger auf Scharhörn*, N, 1927; *Die Hafenorgel*, P, 1937, 1948; *Kadenzen*, P, 1942; *Der große Fluß im Meer*, 1956; *Bordbuch des Satan*, Chronicle, 1959; *Hamburg*, sketchbook, 1962; *River in the Sea*, 1957, Putnam, N.Y.

MECKEL, Christoph. Born 1935 in Berlin. Fled to the West in 1945. Graphic artist, poetry, prose. Three books of etchings. *Nebelhörner*, P, 1959; *Tarnkappe*, P, 1961; *Land der Umbramauten*, P, 1961; *Wildnisse*, P, 1962.

MIEGEL, Agnes. Born 1879 in Königsberg, East Prussia, where she lived till she fled to the West in 1945. Journalist, novelist, and poet. Lives in Nenndorf. *Gesammelte Werke*, VI vols., 1952-55.

NEUMANN, Gerhard. Born 1928 in Rostock. Drafted at 16. Prisoner of war till 1946. Bus driver, miner, teacher. Now a free-lance writer in Wiesbaden. *Wind auf der Haut*, P, 1956; *Salziger Mond*, P, 1958.

PIONTEK, Heinz. Born 1925 Upper Silesia, has been living in West Germany since the war. Now a free-lance writer. Dillingen/Danube. Translations of Keats. Poetry, radio plays, essays. *Die Rauchfahne*, P, 1953/56; *Wassermarken*, P, 1957; *Weißer Panther*, RP, 1962; *Mit einer Kranichfeder*, P, 1962, *Kastanien aus dem Feuer*, Sst, 1963.

RAEBER, Kuno. Born 1922 Klingnau, Switzerland. Has been living in Switzerland, France, Germany, now in Munich. *Gesicht am Mittag*, P, 1950; *Die verwandelten Schiffe*, P, 1957; *Die Lügner sind ehrlich*, N, 1960; *Flußufer*, P, 1963.

SACHS, Nelly. Born 1891 in Berlin, fled to Stockholm in 1940, where she is still living. *In den Wohnungen des Todes*, P, 1947; *Und niemand weiß weiter*, P, 1957; *Fahrt ins Staublose*, P, 1961.

SCHARPENBERG, Margot. Born 1924 in Cologne. Librarian. Has been living in Canada and New York for several years. *Gefährliche Übung*, P, 1957; *Spiegelschriften*, P, 1961.

SCHRÖDER, Rudolf Alexander. Born 1878 Bremen. Died in 1962. Co-founder of *Die Insel*, 1899. Outstanding representative of the European classical and Protestant tradition. Translations from English, French, Greek, Latin, Dutch. (Homer, Vergil, Cicero, Shakespeare, Molière, T. S. Eliot, etc.) 27 books of poetry. *Gesammelte Werke*, VII vols. 1952-'63.